"Clif and Dave were the very first people who inspired me to dream big. Clif is one of the most talented entrepreneurs I've met. On top of his talent ,he has passion for personal development, consistent work ethic and priceless experiences he documented in this book. He is an industry leader and everyone could learn something from Clif."

Danny Bae – ACN

Words really can't describe the talent Clif has in this industry. I worked with him early in my career, which was a major piece in formulating my foundation. A foundation that has helped lead to all the success I have achieved the past decade. I have no doubt that his book will be insightful and helpful to many...

Duke Tubtim -Ariix

"Clif is one the most naturally gifted network marketers I've known. He has been an instrumental part of my success in this industry, and it's great that he is sharing his years of experience through this book. I'm positive the information in this book will change someone else's life as it has mine" - Daniel Song -Yoli

"This book is a do NOT miss!!! Clif Braun is one of the most amazing people I have ever seen in this business!! There's a saying; "Those who can, do. Those who can't, teach!" He does IT, he leads by example and he builds massive teams wherever he goes!! Learn from someone who is doing exactly what he teaches. What a concept! Clif not only one of the best leaders in this business, he is also one of the most caring people I've ever met. He will make you laugh. What he's been through & OVERCOME will make you cry. THANK YOU CLIF...FOR YOUR LEADERSHIP, YOUR VISION, AND MOST OF ALL YOUR FRIENDSHIP! THANK YOU FOR BEING YOU!" Michelle Barnes - VEMMA

Wealth Creation. His systems and methods have helped people make money around the World in multiple time zones and languages. This book is a blue print that Clif has used to live a life very few people will ever get a chance to experience. If you are serious about taking control of your future you need to read this book.

Wes Melcher#1 Best Selling Author on Direct Sales and Network Marketing

Clif Braun is one of the most genuine people I've ever had the chance of meeting. He truly cares about people & wants to help others achieve a high level of success. This book is kick ass, & so is Clif!!!
Alex Morton - VEMMA

"so many people right now want to win. so many people right now want to achieve their goals and dream. This book I believe is a roadmap for anyone who wants to achieve their dreams in life."
Timothy Herr (Master distributor for seacret direct)

I met Clif when he was 19 and it was very obvious he was special. He already displayed a magnetic personality and a natural gift to touch people in a profound way. Clif is very ambitious and I believe whatever he puts his heart into, he will always have success. He does nothing mediocre, but strives to make a significant impact on humanity in a positive way."
Dennis Wong Founder and Owner of YOR

Clifton took my money AND my girl. And yet I am STILL impressed by his skin and his hair. What do u use man?!? WTF? Someone hold me and tell me I will be as smooth as him one day...
Skyler Stone Actor Comedian

"Clif Braun's story is so powerful, so energizing, so inspiring and most importantly so very real! You will be lifted up through his incredible experiences in our industry to realize the simple fact --- "I can do this!" This is a book that every person who has a sincere desire to improve must read!"
Tom Alkazin - VEMMA

Clif Braun is one of the most incredible human beings I have ever met. Super funny, successful, so down to earth and truly super likeable. Admired and envied by so many. Clif Braun u legend.
Graedon Boswell

Preface

Before we get started let's talk about the title, Social Marketing. I think MLM and Network Marketing have become titles that people look at with apprehension. The world is changing, business models evolve and the old school MLM image is dying. Wearing a suit and tie and doing home meetings is old school and nobody wants to do that anymore. These days young people want to wear jeans and a t-shirt, not have a boss and make good money from home. They want their independence. It's not about fancy watches and bling. That's a pitch from the 90's that has given way to a deeper resolve, a resolve to be we and take back control of our lives. We want our dignity. We don't want to be written up and lectured by someone for being 5 minutes late to a job we hate. There is a whole new era of marketers coming out who don't look like, act like or talk like they used to. It's a breath of fresh air and a much needed upgrade for our industry. With that being said, let me tell you how this book began.

I was in Malaysia with my best friend and business partner, Matt Morrow, when I decided to write this book. We were there for a convention, standing in the lobby waiting for Hazrul and Salehin to pick us up. There were three racks of books on personal development and even a few on Social Marketing.

Matt and I started picking up the books and looking at the authors and Matt said, "Half these guys never even made any money in Social Marketing!"

I think out of the six Social Marketing books that were there, he knew five of the authors well. He told me how much money they made in Social Marketing and how much they made from the book and I was blown away. Most of the people writing training books for the Social Marketing industry are getting rich off of us and never even made BIG money in Social Marketing. Matt pointed out to me that I've built bigger teams and made more money than 90% of the people writing these books. More importantly, why are we buying books from people that never hit it BIG even once in Social Marketing? How do they even know what it takes if they haven't done it themselves?

I really should have written this book a

long time ago but it's funny when your business is booming, who has time to write a book? My Social Marketing career has been so exciting and crazy for the past 17 years. I've been the star of the show, the guy on stage, starting a company, leading a company or fighting with the government. I've been sued, lied to, conned, ripped off, pushed out and in, you name it, and I'm still in the game 24/7 and as excited as ever!

For those of you that don't know me my name is Clif Braun and this book is all about showing you that anyone can go from Zero to Hero. I'm not the best and I haven't made the most, but I have hit it BIG in Social Marketing in four different companies. How big? Over $100K a month, meetings twice a week with 1,000 people every Tuesday and Thursday, trainings in convention centers with 9,000 people. At 21, I bought my first Lamborghini in cash, then another one at 23. I moved into the Hollywood Hills above Tobey Maguire and Keanu Reeves. I lived in the Mondrian Hotel on Sunset Blvd for 6 months just for fun. I've traveled and spoken to audiences of thousands all over the world and shared the stage with the best of the best.

Even though I have hit it big almost every year for the past 17 years, my biggest accomplishment is the leaders that have spun off from my team. Many of these leaders are doing better than I am today, and for that I'm so very proud. I'm not a hero, I never was, I just helped people see that it's possible. Over the next few chapters I'm going to tell you my story, give you tips and tricks, training, advice on how to climb to the top, what to do and what *not* do.

I don't believe in holding back, so I use people's names, good and bad. In fact let's name some people right now. Here are a few people that I'm very proud of: Daniel K. Song, Duke Tubtim, Aaron Din, Danny Bae, the twins, Keri and Leisha, Martin Ruholf, and many more I'll mention in later chapters. If I can do it and they can do it, you can do it.

My goal in this book is to share my experiences with you in an effort to get you to understand that we were all nowhere before we got somewhere, and you can and will make it if you want it bad enough.

Table of Contents

Chapter 1
My Story

Yes, I have made a lot of money in Social Marketing and for some reason my brother and I seem to be most famous for driving Lamborghinis. But before all that we were just 2 broke, ambitious kids with a lot of energy.

I was born in Provo, Utah July 12, 1977. My brother was born 1 year later in Carmel, CA on August 10th. Our parents married young, so they struggled financially, but we had a great childhood. I think a lot of successful people out there have more dramatic stories than mine, but the cool thing about my story is it's not too different from most people's stories, probably yours. Well, at least the start isn't.

We grew up in San Jose, CA and I think my brother and I were the only 2 white kids in school. Later, when we moved to Irvine in Orange County, CA, it was way nicer than San Jose.

Our parents asked us how we liked it and we said, "We hate it!"

When they asked us why we didn't like it, we said, "In San Jose we were all broke, but here we're the only kids that are broke!"

We always had the things we needed, but not always the things we wanted. Everyone had brand name stuff like Nike, Quiksilver, Gotcha, while my brother and I had Mervyn's Target and Cheetah, LOL! I know money is not the most important thing in the world, but when you're a kid, fitting in is key, and wearing the right stuff was top priority for me.

My brother Dave and I were always doing something to make extra money. I think our first business venture was in 5th grade. We bought plain, black shirts and then with puffy paint we made fake brand name clothes and sold them in school at recess. Everyone knew we made them so we weren't fooling anyone. The kids at school just liked the shirts we made.

Our dad would take us to Chinatown in Los Angeles every once in a while and we would buy boxes of "bang snaps". Bang snaps are little pieces of paper filled with sand and gravel as a buffer, with a tiny amount of silver fulminate high explosive, so when you throw them on the ground they make a big, snap sound. We bought them in large boxes and sold them in little packages at school until one of the teachers said we couldn't do it anymore. I didn't understand why we couldn't sell stuff during recess! This was the first, but not the last time someone in authority would try to stop us from making money.

My brother and I were not deterred, however. We walked dogs, detailed cars, delivered newspapers, sold magazine subscriptions and even tried telemarketing. We were always doing something so we could get the stuff we wanted. After my parents divorced, my mom would usually say she'd pay for half of whatever we wanted if we could earn the other half on our own. This was the rule for as long as I can remember, from skateboards to bikes, all the way up to our first cars in high school. I think our upbringing played a huge part in our Social Marketing success; we learned that things were not out of reach if you worked for them.

We did well in school until high school. Then, we were so into trying to be popular we spent most of our time hanging out with our friends. We were not really the popular kids, but we hung out in the popular crowd. I guess you could call us wannabes. We wanted to be in the "in" crowd and we kind of were but only because we followed. I think this also played a big role in our future Social Marketing success. We were popular enough to have a little confidence, but not so popular that when Social Marketing was presented to us we would be too busy or too cool to join.

I would say the only tough part of our childhood was when I was 13 and our parents got divorced. They remarried when I was 15, and divorced again when I was 16. This was hard on all of us not just emotionally but also financially. My dad kept the house, and my brother, my mom and I moved into low-income housing so we could stay in Irvine because the schools were good. Both my parents were great people they were just too different. My mom liked to go for walks on the beach, hug a tree and write poems and my dad liked computers and TV.

I was recruited the same way so many of us were, by an annoying friend. I worked at a video arcade center my sophomore year in high school. There was a guy who also worked there from my rival high school. He was kind of weird, lived with his mom as I did, but he didn't have any brothers or sisters, at least none I knew about. I remember I went to his place once after work and it was so dirty it freaked me out, but I was bummed out about a girl I liked and he knew her, so we went back to his apartment and drank shots of warm tequila. I remember thinking to myself, "Wow, this guy is a real loser!" and I left. He was one year younger than me and not in the cool crowd. That's all I really knew about him.

A couple of years later he started calling me like every week trying to get me to go to a "meeting". I kept making up excuses of why I couldn't go or dropping the phone or just even hanging up on him sometimes. He called me for like six months.

Then I started to hear rumors that he was actually making money. My roommate at the time said he was going to go check it out, but I talked him out of it. Finally one night he called me from a blocked number and I answered. He said he would come pick me up the next day for the meeting. I gave in and said fine, just to get him to stop calling me.

I remember how bummed out I was the next day remembering that I had promised him I would go. It felt like a huge weight on my shoulders. He picked me up and he was wearing a grey suit. I couldn't believe he was wearing a suit! Those of you that know me know that by now I'm talking about my first sponsor in Social Marketing, Mr. Tim Herr.

I wanted to change and put on something nicer, but he insisted we would be late and for me not to worry about it, so we walked to his car. When we got to his car it was nothing fancy, but it was new and clean. I remember him driving his other car and it was the ugliest car I had ever seen! It was three different colors, I forget what model, maybe a Toyota Celica or something, but it was like 20 years old. When we got in his new car that night, it was clean and he was listening to motivational tapes. I couldn't believe Tim Herr was in a new, clean car wearing a suit, listening to self-help audio books. He was like a totally different person! Today, Tim Herr is a multimillionaire and one of the top trainers in the industry. We remain good friends and I will always be thankful he got me into Social Marketing. I probably learned 80% of what I needed to get rich from Tim.

When we got to the building I was impressed. It was a huge office and very nice. We were the first ones there. I could tell I was way under dressed in my jeans, t-shirt and skateboarding shoes with a hole in the right shoe. I remember being pissed at Tim for not letting me change. We were way early. He was still new at this time and wasn't perfect yet, but he did get me there.

He walked me around the building and kept pointing to pictures on the wall of people that were high up in the company and telling me their stories. I kept asking him what they all did and what did he do, but he wouldn't tell me. He would only say it was a telecom company. Finally, more people arrived and I was really embarrassed that I was dressed so casually. Everyone else was wearing a suit.

We took a guided tour by a guy who showed us the billing facility and head computer room; he claimed it was built by NASA or something. We finished the tour and finally went into the main room, which held about 500 people and sat down. By the time the meeting started, the room was full. I was a 19-year-old kid in jeans and a t-shirt. Who would have known that I would become the next big thing in this company? Nobody would have bet on me, a punk kid who liked to skateboard, surf, and play video games, living in a tiny, low-income apartment.

The speaker that day was a guy named Paul Myers from Hawaii, a white guy, kind of fat, and laid back. The company was called NTC, which stood for National Telephone and Communications. They made two simple points:

1. Working a job takes all your time and makes too little money.
2. Starting a traditional business is expensive and risky.

This was the first time I was introduced to the concept of recruiting and building a sales team that I would earn overrides on. They said we didn't need any experience and we would get paid exactly what we earned, whatever we produced. All I could think about was how cool this was. I really felt and still do feel it's the most ingenious system in the world.

It was different. It was outside the box. I would have no boss, no hours, and unlimited income. I was so excited!

But I didn't want to show it. I tried to act cool; my vision of a smart businessman was someone who never smiled or showed emotion. When the meeting was over Tim turned to me and asked me what I thought. I told him I thought it looked cool, but I don't have $695.00 to join. He then asked me if I could get it. I said I'd ask my parents, but if they won't help me, I don't think I can join. It's funny how limited my thinking was then and how differently I think now.

He drove me home and I called my dad. It took me 2 weeks to get him to go to a meeting with me, but once he did he joined and loaned me the money to join under him. I was so excited and nervous. We got our kits and went home. There was a bonus of $500.00 for any new person that could recruit 5 other new people in their first month and Tim said he would give me another $500.00 if I did it. My mission was simple, get 12 customers, people to switch their long distance phone service, recruit 5 other people to join like me and help make sure they get 12 customers each, and then duplicate that.

I remember the math so well 5-25-125-625-3,125-15,625-78,125 reps each with 12 customers = like $100K a month or something – It seemed too easy!

I remember looking around the room and thinking to myself, "Wow, if I get 5 and they get 5 and so on and so on, I will fill this whole room in weeks!" I didn't fill it in weeks and it wasn't as easy as I thought it would be, but I ended up doing way more than just filling a room with 500 people.

My brother and I started with nothing and got up to $20K a month our first year in Social Marketing, we earned our first million at age 21 and 22 and were multimillionaires the next year. I remember when we were invited to a party for the top Social Marketing earners in America hosted by Mr. Stuart Johnson. You had to make over $10 million to get invited. My brother and I were so excited. We got dressed up ready to meet the top players in the industry and when we got there, some guy handed me his finished drink thinking I was a waiter! Ouch!

I think that was a big reason we bought Lamborghinis. We were very young and we looked even younger, but the cars really helped us get people's attention. After a zillion people tell you Social Marketing won't work, buying a Lambo and driving back to all their houses was very satisfying. And we did that...a lot! Money and cars were what got our attention back then.

The first 5 people I recruited were my brother, then my girlfriend at the time, Lisa, a pretty blonde Southern California girl I met in Newport Beach, then their family friend, Justin I think was his name, a very nice guy who had overcome many challenges, then Gene Galindo, my old boss from In-N-Out Burger, a Hispanic guy who grew up in Santa Ana in a rough neighborhood. There was also a Chinese girl I met at Kinkos. She was applying for a job and I was there making copies of credibility props for presentations. I waited until she was done talking to the manager and I asked her if she wanted to come visit our office. I told her that we were looking for people and she said, "Yes!" I think her name was Joanna.

Now these first 5 people are all no longer with me, but they helped me get going and I appreciate them all. The world is full of luck, good and bad and I have to say I have had my share of both. I got my 5 and I got them fast. There was some luck involved, although I did go through a lot of people to get those first 5 and to tell you the truth they are not the 5 that I thought would join. My best friends were the ones I thought would join and none of them did; which was an important lesson in itself.

I can still remember making my list. The company I was with, NTC, had a nice little tool that really helped me make it. It was called a memory jogger, which you can find in chapter 5 of this book. A memory jogger basically helps you expand the list of people you could think of to invite to meetings. Using this tool, my first list was 168 names exactly. I got 5 to join. If you are not afraid of getting a few no's, getting 5 isn't hard at all. I was so excited to succeed and so afraid to fail. It was a powerful combination.

Joanna, the Asian girl I signed was very tall, from a wealthy family, and very shy. I thought she would never sign a soul, but she called me the day after she joined and said, "I got someone."

I said, "Great! A guest to come to the next meeting?"

She said, "No, my roommate is ready to join and pay the $695.00."

I was shocked and actually shaking with excitement when she read me the credit card info over the payphone. I was at the UCI Campus, trying to recruit more people. It's funny, the people you think will join never do, and the people you think won't, do. Then the people you think are going to kill it, don't, and the people you think will whine and complain shine like the North Star.

17 years full time and I still can't tell for sure who will fail and who will do well. My best advice to you is not to pre-judge, because when you meet people you only meet the surface. People are like icebergs; there is way more going on in their life than you know. People I thought had it all together were falling apart, people that I thought were losers would spring into action. Social Marketing is very interesting. When people are provided with the opportunity to better themselves they will tell you how bad things are, so you will help them more and connect with them, and it works. I am a bleeding heart, the people that opened up to me and shared their fears are the ones I really fought for. I had my pains and I shared them with everyone, not like complaining, but more like relating so people could feel me.

So Lisa enrolled her family. Gene

Galindo showed up with 9 guests his first night and signed 5 of them. Joanna faded away after enrolling 2 people. Lisa faded away after her team got up to about 30 people. Gene's team exploded through fellow In-N-Out employees, but my brother only had a few people in. Then one night we went to dinner at Black Angus in our new Armani Suits. Our first check we spent on suits and we had $0 left after, but we each had 1 Armani Suit!

We strutted into the restaurant. When we were seated, we proudly folded our suits label side out, hoping the waiter would notice and ask us what we did. But, he didn't. I'm sure he'd seen plenty of nice suits. At any rate, he was definitely not impressed.

It was getting late and the restaurant was closing. Dave and I were about to leave when a bus boy walked by. He noticed the suits and asked us what we did. We told him we were in telecom and that our company was actually looking for some more people. He came to a meeting a few days later. His name was Chris Yee, a student at UCI. He joined right away and enrolled a few people, one of which was a kid named Alex Chi Ku Qua, a Taiwanese kid with influential parents. He joined and took it so seriously he started wearing Armani suits to school…high school! He failed gym because he wouldn't take off his suit!

This kid was smart. His mom taught piano lessons to a little girl whose parents were super rich, Laurdus and Chatri Junjuwala. They owned a company called Time Plus, Inc. They sold $10.00 watches all over the world. Chatri was Indian, but spoke Chinese and English. I believe Laurdus was South American. Anyway, Alex told his mom to tell Chatri she would give her free piano lessons if Chatri would go to a meeting with Alex. Chatri said "Sure!"

So a few days later Dave and I were standing outside the office on Main and Jamboree and all of a sudden we saw a black Mercedes-Benz S600 pull in and we saw Alex was sitting in the back! He brought Chatri! Chatri joined and started signing up everyone he knew, his friends his family, his employees. He even gave me his red SL500 convertible Mercedes to drive around to help us recruit more people so he could reach the Director Position. Amazing huh? My brother couldn't get 1 person in 3 months, then he gets a bus boy who gets a kid who gets Chatri. Social Marketing is nuts! Never quit because you never know who will end up in your organization.

I feel like you may be wondering why

I'm telling you about these first 5 people. They are not the ones that made me rich, with the exception of my brother who later becomes my partner. It's because your first 5 are your first 5! They are the most exciting people you will ever recruit, the scariest, the most challenging and the most important because this is the first step in getting rich and making it BIG. Everyone had to get their first 5!

Anyone in Social Marketing will tell you that the first step is to know your WHY. Mine was simple. I was tired of watching my mom cry herself to sleep every night, I was tired of looking in the fridge 20 times a day hoping something good would appear. When I would go to my friends' houses they had fridges full of ready-to-eat, processed foods. My mom cooked from scratch, because it was healthier and cheaper. I didn't appreciate that at the time. If I wanted something to eat between meals, she always said, "There's stuff to eat, you just have to make it!"

I was like, "Great! What the hell am I supposed to make with mustard, eggs and cereal?"

I felt bad for my mom and I wanted more out of life, I knew working a job would never give me the lifestyle I wanted but I always planned to graduate from college.

Graduating from college was so etched in my brain I assumed if you didn't you would end up a janitor.

Once I started doing well in my first and second month, my sponsor Tim asked me if I still wanted to go to college. I said even if I had a million dollars right now I would still go to college. It wasn't until I started listening to Jim Rohn that I realized formal education can make you a living, but self-education could make you a fortune. I was so in love with the Social Marketing concept after my first 30 days I quit my job and decided to go full time. I remember standing outside the office talking with Tim and I told him I quit my job. He gave me this shocked look, which freaked me out and I asked him what was wrong. He said "Nothing! That's great! I just never had a full time rep before."

Two things made me successful in Social Marketing:

1. The fear of not making it.
2. The excitement of making it!

Tim was a great coach. None of us knew exactly what we were doing, but Tim kept us all motivated. Eventually I started to really take off and do well. Whether or not it was true, I felt maybe I was a threat to Tim's fame in the company as the young, superstar. He started spending more time with his other teams and less time with me, as he should have, but I was still a little hurt. Shortly thereafter, I ended up meeting a guy who would change my life forever.

It was a Thursday morning; VIP Thursday where all the bigwigs showed up. After the catered lunch, the president of the company, Jerry Ballah, spoke at the end of the meeting, and he was magic. These Thursday mornings were packed! I saw a young man, maybe 34 years old, who looked like a Chinese Richard Gere. He was sitting in the front row with a very pretty Chinese woman and a very pretty African American girl. They were dressed to kill, all black, Armani this and Gucci that, diamond watches and rings, but not too much, still classy. I couldn't take my eyes off them the whole meeting. I kept watching them.

They were dead serious and I liked that. After the meeting, I introduced myself to this young guy. He told me his name was Dennis, the black girl was his fiancée, and the Chinese girl was his sister, Sophia. I asked him for some advice and on what his daily activities were. He said, "Work hard." He smiled, patted me on the shoulder and rushed out with his crew. The next time I saw him I told him I had taken his advice and stepped up my game. He saw something in me I hoped was there, potential, so he started coaching me a little here and there until we became friends.

He told me he was opening his own office in Monterey Park. He told me to break up with my girlfriend, drop out of college and come work with him. He was not in my upline and at the time I didn't understand what a big problem this would cause, but I said YES! I called my mom and told her I was taking a break from college. I broke up with my girlfriend, and my brother and I moved to Monterey Park.

We packed up a U-Haul truck and moved into a property that one of Dennis' downline owned. It was an office that was converted into an apartment. It was small and dirty. We had no hot water, but it was 430 bucks a month. We slept on the floor and had no TV. We listened to Jim Rohn in the U-Haul truck the whole way from Irvine to Monterey Park. Dave and I loved the concept of Social Marketing and we loved listening to Jim Rohn and other motivational speakers, but we had a hard time getting our teams to listen to them. So we made up our minds to memorize everything they said and we would just teach it to our people.

We listened to every word the man said and wrote down every word in our journals.

I can bet you dollars to donuts nobody has Jim Rohn down like we do. Our teams would listen to us but they wouldn't buy the tapes and listen on their own so we became little Jim Rohn prophets and everyone on our team was blown away by our knowledge and ability to speak. Our teams grew because we were listening to great stuff and sharing it daily with our teams.

I think those first 6 months were the scariest and hardest. Teams would rise and then fall, rise and then fall and I started to feel like more people were failing than succeeding. This feeling almost made me quit, but then Tim explained it so well. He said we are giving people a chance. We are giving them a shovel; they have to dig. A personal trainer can only coach you in the gym; he can't do it for you. He explained that most people fail at everything they do and that Social Marketing was no different. He said focus on the people that deserve your help, not the ones that need it, but aren't willing to work.

Maybe 6 or 7 months into my first year I made enough money to buy a new car, a black BMW 5 Series. It's funny because I used to make fun of people that drove nice cars like that, but once I could afford it, I wanted one! After purchasing the car my brother and I drove to Vegas to celebrate.

Only one problem. When we got there we couldn't check into a hotel room because we weren't 21. We spent the night in the car at the MGM parking lot and drove home the next day. We didn't care. We thought it was funny. We could buy a $50K car, but not get a hotel room.

I have to thank my parents here because if it wasn't for them my brother and I couldn't have gotten our first two nice cars. Yeah, we were making money, but we had no credit. Our mom co-signed for our NSX and our dad co-signed for our BMW. Thanks Mom & Dad!

Eventually the drama of me working in LA really upset the OC side of the company and it began a small war that fueled old wars and eventually unraveled the company. I wouldn't say NTC fell apart because of me, but I would say I didn't help resolve any old wounds.

I reached the position of Director, $20K-$30K a month income at 19 years old and I was the 2nd or 3rd fastest person in the company's history to do it. My first weekly check as a Director was $7,624.00. I'll never forget it. I had an "Aha!" moment that they could and would print me big checks if I did big numbers. The lid was raised for me big time that day.

Tim feared I was going to switch under

Dennis so he started moving my teams around which I documented and showed the company. They said I could switch under Dennis, but I had to start all over from scratch and leave my title and all my reps under Tim. On top of this, Dennis was not going to compensate me a penny. All he offered me was teamwork, help, support and mentorship. I felt he should have helped me a little more, but I said OK. I knew long term he was the guy that could help me become the person I wanted to be. He was sharp, classy, smart, tough but fair. I seriously wanted to be him.

Tim really opened the door for me and my brother. He taught me the basics of Social Marketing. He taught me not to major in the minors. He taught me leadership by example and heart. He really was amazing. But at that time, I was young and hungry and Tim and I had very different styles. Tim to me was too rough around the edges. Tim was Humvee and Dennis was a Rolls Royce, which is what he drove by the way.

The years I spent with Dennis were some of the best years of my life. We became like brothers. He coached me, guided me, mentored me, hung out with me, and treated me like an equal. I worked my ass off and took more feedback from him than anyone ever in my entire life. He made me cry on several occasions, but I could feel myself growing so I pressed forward. Dennis said we were going to leave NTC and he was going to start his own company. I said, "Let's go!" We did. It failed. I moved into one of the apartment buildings he owned. He opened another Social Marketing company and it failed. I couldn't pay rent and he evicted me.

I thought he was a jerk and cheap. He said it was tough love. He said we have choices to make and one thing had nothing to do with the other. My car was repossessed, and we had nowhere to live. We were about to give up when as luck would have it Dennis' sister, Sophia Wong broke up with her boyfriend, Jeff Morgan. He didn't want to be alone, so he let us move into his luxury apartment where Dave and I shared a room and slept on the floor.

So there we were, sharing a room, sleeping on the floor. No money, no credit and Jeff says, "I have an idea for us to open another company!"

We came up with the name, the logo, everything. Then he said he was going to pitch it to Dennis and Sophia, but if they gave it the green light Dave and I had to act surprised. They did, we did, and 2by2.net was formed from ashes to one of the fastest growing companies in Social Marketing history. Heck, we were in Inc. Magazine as the 16th fastest growing internet company in America and it started with just Dennis, his sister Sophia, Jeff, and the Braun Brothers.

Dave and I had no car, so we had to get up early in the morning and drop our mom off at school so we could use her Toyota Rav4. We would get up at 5 AM, drop her off at 6 AM, then go do meetings all day and get back at school by 4 PM to pick her up. Then for night meetings we would have our downlines pick us up to take Dave and I to do meetings for them. They didn't mind because Dave and I were helping them build their teams and Dave and I had become good presenters. Most of our little downline were young, broke, Hispanic or Asian kids and from just a few kids we grew an army up to 67,000 people in 8 different legs earning us millions in a few short years. At our peak we were signing up over 5,000 reps a month at 420 bucks and we held that production level for 2 to 3 years.

We started doing meetings in Downey with one of our only active reps at the time Duke Tubtim, a kid that walked into our office on accident looking for a job. That same day he applied for jobs at Best Buy and Jack in the Box. He was with us for almost 2 years before 2by2 started and never made a penny, but when we started 2by2 he got excited. We started doing meetings late at night out of a telemarketing office in the Valley. Soon we outgrew that little office and so we got an office in Downey at a check-cashing place. We took down the sign, painted the office, made it look as nice as we could and then we outgrew that little office.

We started doing hotel meetings in West Covina at the Radisson, which is now the Marriott. It started with just a few people and we got those meetings up to 1,000 people a night. I'm not the most successful person ever in Social Marketing, but Dave and I were 2 of the most famous. We killed it on stage, we bought Lamborghinis, diamond watches, a big house on the hill and we were making over $25K a week, every week. It was amazing. We played Techno music before every meeting. The energy in the room was nuts and the room was filled with almost 100% Asian and Hispanic college students. We all wore suits and ties like Dennis taught us. He's the one that first showed me how to tie a tie and how to use shoetrees, etc.

We would fill convention centers with 9,000 people and rock the house. I know there are bigger companies out there, but this was our baby! We grew it; we did it from Zero to Hero. When the meetings were over people would line up to get us to sign their journal. Sometimes the line would be 100 people long. I remember thinking how silly that was and how awkward it made me feel. I started telling people I would only sign their journal if they signed mine. I have 1,000's of people's signatures now.

Even when Dave and I would go to the mall or the movies people would come up to us and shake our hands. It was weird but exciting. I remember one night we went out and I was in the bathroom stall and someone was trying to talk to me. I thought, "Wow this is what it's like to be famous." It can be annoying.

No privacy! My girlfriend and I were in the car, the orange Lambo, arguing one day and someone ran up to the window and asked how fast it went. They kept asking questions, trying to get me to roll down the window. I wanted to open the door and shout at them, but I rolled down the window, smiled, said 205, and then drove off.

Buying our first Lamborghini was nuts. It was Dennis' first and it was of course the best. It was car #5 of 12 in the world, the fastest, the loudest, the brightest Alpine Momo Edition. When we would pull up to restaurants the attention we got was insane. Then one of our downline, Duke Tubtim bought Sophia's Lambo. We had to twist his arm but he finally agreed. Then another one of our downline got one, then another and another. I think we had 9 Lambo owners on our team. When we drove around together the street rumbled. We even shut down downtown LA and hired a police escort with helicopters so we could make a cool company video. I have to say that to this day many of the young top Social Marketing people in our industry got their start under Dave and me in 2by2. Some of them have even since passed us and are doing incredibly well. People like Danny Bae in ACN and others that have come very close like, Daniel K. Song in Yoli, or the Twins in World Ventures, Martin Ruholf, and many more.

Although many of the top Social Marketing people today were recruited and or trained by Dave and me, they have all grown up and spread their wings. They have new coaches now and that's the way it goes sometimes. There was a time when we were bitter about lost or stolen teams, but if you really have a tight relationship with your team and they are earning and learning with you, then they won't leave.

But it's easy to get comfortable when you're making more money than you know what to do with and you stop spending the quality time you should with your leaders.

And I believe that's the trap Dave and I fell into. We were hanging out with celebs every week, parties every weekend, and we fell out of the zone. Hindsight is 20/20 but when you're in the moment sometimes you are so close to the wall that the writing is just too big for you to see.

Dennis got upset that I was not as focused as I used to be. I, of course, rebelled against him. He then, of course, started trying to reduce my power. Dave and I had become 90% of 2by2. The reps, the employees; everyone looked at Dave and me as 2by2. Originally I named this book Zero to Hero because it was catchy, and that's what people want to do, they want to go to the top, but the truth is you never are a hero. We were never heroes, we were training wheels. We were a stepping-stone in people's learning curve. We were an example. We may have helped or advised, but the only one that can teach you is you. Once you start to buy into your own press you're headed down fast.

OK. Let's talk about some positive things. Whose lives were changed by 2by2? What are some of the success stories? Why? When you see people on stage or in their new car sometimes it just seems so far away, like the journey is too long and challenging. But it's not, it just looks that way. It's a lot closer to you than you think. We became and created millionaires. Let's talk about one of our most famous downlines ever, Mr. Duke Tubtim. I mentioned him earlier when I started talking about our rise to the top but allow me to give you a little background on Mr. Duke. Duke was the quietest, shyest person I had ever met. He ended up making $50K a week and became our top producer, but when I met him he was just a little Thai guy so scared to talk we had to really be patient with him to even have a conversation.

When 2by2 started, Dave and I didn't have cars so Duke would borrow his parents' Honda and pick us up. Then we would go do meetings all over the place - as many as we could as often as we could. I hear people all the time say you have to have a certain type of personality to do well in Social Marketing, but this is not true, not even close. Duke almost never said a word. For his first 6 months in 2by2 I think we did every meeting and training for him. His downlines would sometimes complain to us that they didn't trust him because he was so quiet. We assured everyone he was just a shy guy. We never really understood how smart Duke was until he started making money, gained confidence and started talking. I guess he knew that he didn't know anything and he just wanted to be quiet and watch Dave and me. But once he came out of his shell, he was a beast!

Duke was the best organizational leader I had ever worked with. He planned out everything. I guess he knew motivation was not his strength, so he used calculations, strategy, promotions, impending events, etc. He was always thinking. I remember his parents didn't approve of us hanging out with him so much. His dad was a disabled, aging man who stayed home a lot and kind of freaked me out. Once Duke started making money, his parents warmed up to us. But I think it was more than just the money. Duke was now wearing a suit and tie and listening to personal development. He was not just making more, he was becoming more.

OK, so who were Duke's top people? Maybe 2 of the most memorable for Dave and me were Lazaro and Chepe Gutierrez because they were brothers. Chepe was similar to me in a lot of ways and Lazaro was more like Dave in many ways. Chepe and I are all heart and Laz and Dave help us stay grounded and think. We met Laz and Chep in a church. We had a white board and a tiny little TV that we played a video on before the meeting called "The Buzz", if I remember correctly.

Laz and Chep grew up in South Gate and I remember Duke introduced Dave and I to this tiny audience of like 6 people in this old church. Duke told everyone Dave and I had made a lot of money and we were there to share with them how we did it. I remember thinking, "These guys are going to jump us."

Funny thing is, years later they told us the thought crossed their minds! Lazaro worked for Keebler Cookies stocking shelves and Chepe worked at a bank. They ended up becoming millionaires with us and getting their own Lamborghini, nice homes, watches and all the other goodies us Social Marketing people like to buy once we make it to prove to everyone we made it. Something I later learned is not totally necessary.

Then there was Patty Oh, a Korean girl I met in a bar, which sounds bad, but it's true. Funny thing is she was a total church girl - I mean like super religious. I don't even remember how I signed her up but I do remember she went from shy little church girl driving a little, white car with somewhere around 200K miles on it, to becoming one of the strongest leaders I've ever worked with. She is a real role model for thousands of young women around the country. I worked with her the same way Dave and I worked with all of our reps. We did all the meetings until she could fly on her own and she flew fast.

She would do all her own hotel meetings with her brand new Viper parked outside. We used to always know when Patty Oh was coming because your shirt would shake from her exhaust. When she told me she wanted a Viper, I laughed. I could not picture a little Korean church girl driving a Dodge Viper, but she did it. She really stepped up and hit it BIG and I'll never forget her.

Then there was Dr. Matta and Dr. Luis, 2 people my brother met somewhere and we ended up placing them under Duke. They were something. They named their group "Team Think Big" and they brought a lot of credibility to our team and the company for that matter. These were 2 cool guys. Dr. Matta was a chiropractor with the best attitude of anyone I've ever met. It seems like a lot of chiropractors have that great attitude. He was just the nicest guy, always smiling and positive. He had a great wife and loved being a chiropractor, but like most of us, he wanted more. He saw the success Dave and I were having and like any successful person smelling opportunity, he jumped in.

Dr. Matta never bought a Lamborghini. He did it his own way. He bought a Hummer and made it into the coolest, high tech

40

Hummer the world had ever seen. It's been on TV and in magazines, you name it. He was from Azusa and lived close to our headquarters in City of Industry. His partner, Dr. Luis was a tall man who was really into personal development and seminars. "Team Think Big" became one of the largest groups in the company. They did meetings in doctors' offices and small businesses all over San Gabriel and the Inland Empire. These were the people that really helped get 2by2 going.

2by2.net became one of the fastest growing Social Marketing Companies ever and it happened because we all worked together as a team and followed the vision of Dennis and Sophia. The way to make it BIG in Social Marketing is to work as a team. To this day, 2by2.net is still the company and project I'm most proud of and to this day it's what people remember me for. Even though Dave and I went on to make money in other companies, people still think of Lamborghinis and 2by2.net stickers on cars when they hear the names Clif & Dave. Some people think 2by2.net got shut down, but the truth is it just fell apart.

Chapter 2
Why Social Marketing?

People say a lot of bad things about Social Marketing, but you can say a lot of bad things about any business. Before I talk about why Social Marketing, let's take a look at the world today because it's not the same world in which our parents and grandparents grew up.

The advice and coaching we get is not only outdated, it's also polluted with hidden agendas from the system in which we live. I'm going to ask you to take a step back and look at the big picture. Who created our system? Who is running the show? Sometimes we can't see the reality in which we are living. In America and in just about every country, it's the rich people that are running the show. The system is designed to keep them rich and to keep you working for them.

If you don't believe me, just look at our tax system. The rich pay less in taxes than you do! I know because I had a job and then got rich in Social Marketing and the percentage I paid after getting rich was lower than what I paid when I was broke. If you own property there are tax benefits. If you own a business you get tax write-offs. If you have a job, you will pay more.

Even Warren Buffet believes this is wrong! We grow up hearing sayings like "stinking rich". But why does being rich stink? We grow up hearing money is "cold hard cash." No, it's not! Money is warm and fuzzy! We have grown up thinking you have to be ruthless to make a lot of money, but that's not true. Some people make it that way, but not everyone does.

There's a scripture that is often misquoted. It's not "MONEY is the root of all evil.", but "The LOVE of money is the root of all evil." Money for its own sake is a shallow goal, but you can do a lot of good things with money. It's a tool, a means to an end, and can be used for so much good.

We spend 14,000 hours in school learning how to complete assignments, be on time, listen, take direction, pay attention, don't step out of line, graduate, and get a degree. We're promised this will ensure us a better life, a high paying job, and social status. The system is designed to breed employees. If you go to a nice college, get a degree and a good job, everyone looks at you as a success, a normal, good person.

Whether or not they went to college, billionaires and millionaires all over the world got that way from starting their own businesses. We are taught over and over again to start at the bottom as an employee and work our way up. That works sometimes, but many business owners didn't do that. They started a business, so they started at the top and then they built the bottom.

Sound familiar? Social Marketing works like that. You start at the top of your company and you build the bottom. In the beginning there is nothing, but you build it just like a company starts!

CORPORATE AMERICA TREE DIAGRAM

The regular system is not designed for you and me. The system is designed for us to live by the bell, living for the weekend.

Sound familiar? Don't get me wrong. I'm not trying to bash all jobs, but as we've learned with the recent economic recession, jobs do not equal financial security.

Security is what drives people to work at jobs they don't like, but I think having a job is scarier than working for commission. When you have a job you are dependent on one source of income. If you are working for commission you are in full control of your income. If you get many customers, you have many sources of income. I feel more stable and secure this way, but that's my personality. I'm always amazed that people settle for less, and then complain about it. So many people are working in jobs where they make barely enough to pay their bills. They can never go on vacations, save money, or just go shopping and spoil themselves. They can't donate to charities or help others financially. But when you offer them a way to change it, they hug the false security of their jobs tighter!

Only 40% of the population has the capacity to be successful at Social Marketing, or at owning any business. You can't make a duck an eagle and there is nothing wrong with ducks! Don't get a big ego just because you are doing well in a commission-based business. I respect people holding down jobs that help our society.

Some of the noblest people I have met have low paying jobs, but they truly make a difference in this world. It's just sad to see the system doesn't take care of, or care about these people. Police, Firemen, Teachers and Environmentalists are the unsung heroes that the system doesn't pay enough; people like my mom, who teaches 6th graders and makes a HUGE difference in the formative years of our future leaders.

When I talk about why you should do Social Marketing, it's from the point of view assuming that you want to get out of the rat race and get ahead in life. There are many ways to make a living, many ways to get ahead and many ways to make a difference. Social Marketing is not the only way and it may not be for you! It takes a lot of mental toughness, desire and inner strength. Some people aren't up for it and that's OK. But understand that there are challenges everywhere. Police risk their lives and for not much money. Teachers are blamed for the nation and the family's failures and doctors get sued all the time. So if you think Social Marketing is risky I invite you to take a look around the world and consider your options. I'm convinced 1000% that Social Marketing is the best way, the most logical, and the most fun with the least risk.

Society has frowned on Social Marketing

because society has a mob mentality. Who influences our opinions? The media, mainly. Who controls the media? The rich! Who wants you to stay an employee and in their system working for them? The rich!

The rich create and control the system and our opinions through movies, TV, the news, radio... AKA mainstream media. The one thing you can be sure of is that what you think you know is tainted. The information you get on the news is the opinion of that station, or whoever owns the station, or at least it's polluted with it. Few news programs even pretend to be objective anymore.

So as we look at the big picture, it's obvious that there is a system at work, but it's not designed for you or me to become the next owner of Johnson & Johnson. It's designed for you and me to become a part of their work force. They will pat us on the head and may give us $100K a year. We may be able to buy a nice car and house with that salary, but then we will be slaves to our bills and never be able to open a business or compete with the BIG guys.

We've all heard these two sayings so often; we think they are true:

"The rich get richer, and the poor get poorer."

"It takes a lot of money to make a lot of money."

These are limiting beliefs that have been driven into our heads, but they don't have to be true. You can get rich and you can start from nothing. That's how many of the super rich people got there. You just have to get out of the system. You have to start your own business, which leads us to the second reason you should do Social Marketing. 95% of small businesses fail in the first 3-5 years, many much sooner.

Now, before I get into this, let's quickly recap the first reason. The system is designed for us to work for them and that's reason enough to make me want to get rich outside the system. It's unfair and it's deceptive. If reason #1 isn't enough for you, then think about this. Let's say you do start a small business. The Small Business Administration says it now costs an average of $100K to start a small business and 95% of them will fail.

First off, where are you going to get the $100K from? Second, if you got the $100K now you have to risk it and be able to run the business and not take a check for 1-5 years until it's profitable. You have made back your $100K, but now you are just

48

even! In this economy that's not a smart move. I don't know about you, but I don't like those odds.

I know a woman who wanted to join Social Marketing, but the next day was made fun of by her shallow, celebrity friends in LA. So she quit Social Marketing and opened a very cool coffee shop. Her friends hung out there all the time. Everyone wanted to be her friend because she owned the cool coffee shop in a great part of Hollywood, but her hours were insane, her employees didn't respect her, and she didn't have a coach to help her through it. It cost her $200K to get this little shop open, it was $200K that was borrowed from friends and family who would not support her in Social Marketing but loved the idea of her starting a cool coffee shop. In less than a year she was out of business.

I remember walking to her shop and being shocked that everything was gone, the store was empty. In less than 1 year she lost $200K. Her family and friends that she borrowed the money from don't talk to her anymore and she is now back in school to get her master's degree. To get her master's will cost her more in student loans because she can't borrow it from her family now.

People say they have lost money or friends in Social Marketing. Pshhhhhh!

People can and do lose money and friends doing any business, the difference is with Social Marketing you can lose a few hundred bucks, but with traditional businesses you can lose hundreds of thousands or more.

Now let's look at Social Marketing. You can join any decent Social Marketing company for a few hundred dollars like I did at 19. You can get your income up way past a small business owner like I did in Social Marketing as a teenager! Trust me I'm no genius; if I can do it you can do it. In Social Marketing your startup fee is small, but your earning potential is HUGE! In a small business you have to rely on yourself and there is nobody to coach you through it. You have employees, payroll, small business laws, rules and regulations, insurance problems, rent, stock and more. In Social Marketing, you have a sponsor who only makes money when you do, so he or she wants to help you. If he or she is unhelpful, you can find someone above them in your upline to help you. If a company doesn't work out, you lost a few hundred bucks and you live to fight another day. Just make sure you save your money when you make it.

Social Marketing makes so much sense. It blows my mind that people are still skeptical. Warren Buffet owns Social

Marketing companies, Donald Trump endorses Social Marketing, President Clinton has endorsed Social Marketing, Robert Kiyosaki, the famous author of "*Rich Dad, Poor Dad*" heavily endorses Social Marketing. Countless celebrities are in Social Marketing, many of which I have personally enrolled. Yes, I'm bragging now.

I have signed up so many doctors and attorneys that have told me how much they envy my lifestyle. Historically, people are envious of doctors and lawyers; but with their titles come a lot of problems I don't have. If someone wants to sue, they sue the company, not me. I don't have a boss, but I have upline support and customer service support. I can come and go as I please; I can work in over 50 countries because the company I'm involved with operates in more than 50 countries. I have lived a lifestyle that most people only see on TV or read about in magazines and I did it my way, outside the system.

I have always wanted to live in Asia and I made it happen. I have thousands of reps all over the world, reps in Canada, India, America, Europe, Japan, Malaysia, Singapore, Taiwan and now, Africa. What's so cool about Social Marketing is you can get rich and be unknown!

When I go to our conventions in different

countries and speak, I get to dress up, wear a suit and tie, speak on stage and be a total rock star. After a training I will sign autographs and take pictures with people for over an hour. But when the convention is over I get to go back home and be unknown again. I always thought it would be cool to be famous, but after hitting it big in Social Marketing I realize being famous would not be fun. The cool part of Social Marketing is I get to taste fame, but I don't have to live with it.

I remember speaking for 2,000 people in Malaysia with Matt Morrow and Darren Hardy from Success Magazine. We were done talking and the day was through. We couldn't go to Starbucks or the lobby or the valet or anywhere with out taking a zillion pictures with reps. We are all used to it now, but I remember when I first hit it BIG in Social Marketing - it was crazy.

When people look up to you so much that they will skip work, buy a plane ticket and fly to another country just to hear your training, it really puts a lot of responsibility on your shoulders. Social Marketing has made me a better person and it has made me realize what life is all about. Life is all about helping other people.

I'm happiest when I'm learning, teaching and growing. Life for me now is about sharing my experiences with people to inspire them and help them see that success is not as far away as they think it is. The greatest part about Social Marketing is the mentorship. It's the training and support you receive from people that are where you want be. I have never seen a traditional corporation with better training and support system than a good Social Marketing company.

Some people think a franchise is a safe bet to take to kind of ease into owning your own business, without taking all the risks; but even if you open a franchise you are still not guaranteed success. Yes, the training and support is there but many people have invested their life savings into franchises only to see them crash and burn. There are no guarantees in life. I always look at the risk vs. the reward, and in Social Marketing the risk is so small but the reward can be MASSIVE.

Another thing I don't think enough people understand and appreciate is the fact that you don't need to feel awkward once you are making a lot of money in Social Marketing. When I hang around people that are not making the money that I am, I take great pride in the fact that I can offer them the exact if not better opportunity than I had. I can help them, I can coach them, and I can make a difference. If you are an actor, basketball player or doctor, and your friends don't make the money you do, then there is awkwardness present. I never feel that because I was where they were and I found a better way. My day-to-day is helping people make it, so I'm very comfortable in any crowd.

Chapter 3
How to Choose the Right Company

First off, you have to choose a company that fits your personality. In my twenties I only represented companies with a high tech or a dot com image, because I couldn't see myself pushing diet pills or shakes to my friends. I couldn't see myself packing the trunk of my car and trying to sell skin care to my friends. My generation was more into MP3's and online shopping, Internet access and online travel, fame and fortune, so I aligned myself with companies that projected the image to which I knew my demographic would respond.

If you are not into what you are promoting, you won't be good at it for long. We have all heard the saying, "It's not what you say that's important, it's how you feel about what you say that matters."

I'm here to tell you this is so true. Jim Rohn says words are like a needle. Throw a needle at someone and see if it affects them, but weld that needle to an iron bar and then poke someone with it gently and boy, will they feel it! The iron bar behind the pin is the emotion behind your words that can't be faked. If you really feel strong about something, others will see that. The last 4 letters of the word enthusiasm stand for I Am Sold Myself. If you believe, they will believe. If you have doubts, they will have doubts.

I have seen people with very few contacts and very little talent make big money in Social Marketing, and I have seen burned-out, industry leaders that stand by and watch these talentless newbies smoke them in production.

People make their decisions based on 20% logic and 80% emotion. Don't take it from me, watch any car commercial: "…adrenaline, speed…!" Or how about a jeans commercial featuring sultry girls revealing flat, bare stomachs. The commercial is 80% about how you feel and 20% about the quality of the jeans or even less. This is done because ad agencies know you buy based on emotion not facts. The funny thing is we sit back and make fun of these commercials and we feel they are an insult to our intelligence, and the ad agencies sit back and look at their research on what we respond to and laugh all the way to the bank.

There is some silly car commercial with the directions to their dealership in a jingle. I may never go there, but I have never forgotten how to! "605 to South Street... Cerritos Auto Square!" We are way simpler than we think we are. So the first thing you need to understand is that you need to be really into the company, the product or service, and that your belief system is so crucial to your success. If you are not really into what you're doing, you won't last very long and you won't be able to move others. I have been in a few different companies and I can tell you I did well in all of them because I believed in all of them.

What's interesting is that we choose to follow people that are sincere. We don't know if they are right or not, but studies show we follow people that are certain, over people that are uncertain. Jim Rohn says it best, "Sincerity is not a good test of right or wrong, a person can be very sincere but be sincerely wrong." Unfortunately there are so many confident, broke morons out there we tend to listen to them!

So understand that if you really want people to follow you, it's imperative that you believe in what you're doing. People lie, but body language doesn't, and whether it is conscious or unconscious, we can all read body language. If you get a funny feeling about someone, it is probably their body language. According to UCLA professor, Dr. Mehrabian's research, only 7% of our communication is verbal, 55% is body language and 38% tonality.

You need to find a company with a product or service you really believe in, in an industry that you are excited about it!

Second, you need to understand timing of the market. Is this product or service long term? Is it a fad? Is it not well received by the government? What's the track record of companies that promoted this product or service? These are all important questions. If the product is a fad that may be OK if the company has plans to launch a new product or service every six months, if that is what that industry requires.

Technology becomes outdated every 6 months, so if it's a service the company is providing, what are their future plans? I have made most of my money in service based, dot com, Social Marketing companies, but I do not recommend them. With the exception of a few companies, the majority of the money in service based companies or online shopping is made from people joining vs. a physical product. The money made from online shopping is so small, but the money made from people joining is large. It is in these types of companies you can make big money fast, but they never last.

The government will shut them down for being a pyramid, because the money is made from signup fees not the services. Trust me, I know. If they are not shut down and they get big, their plan is always to have an exit strategy to sell the company to Google or whatever dot com company has an interest. The big dot com companies have a business model and it is to buy out all threats. BurnLounge was an amazing Social Marketing company, 2by2.net was an amazing Social Marketing company, but the government doesn't like non-product based companies. Simple as that.

Now there are always exceptions to the rules, A.C.N. is a huge success, Danny Bae, one of their top leaders has been with them for years and built an empire. I admire the leadership and cutting edge technology of ACN. They have done a lot for the credibility of our industry. But just remember, most service based companies, especially the startups, don't last very long. With that being said, rules are made to be broken and I admire the people that break them and win against all odds.

Every travel Social Marketing Company has been shut down or failed with the exception of World Ventures, a company that has lasted beyond everyone's expectations. I believe the success of World Ventures is due primarily to one man, Marc Accetta. The company was under funded, poorly managed and did not follow their own rules. The leadership of Marc Accetta and his training program is what turned the company around. I was there in the beginning at a very high level. In fact it was Mike, Wayne my brother and I that decided to start World Ventures together. I remember picking up Marc Accetta and his wife from the airport squeezing them into my Ferrari when they first decided to become a part of World Ventures. To make a very long story short 2 of our reps left our team and joined a different team in World Ventures, something we all agreed would not be allowed. Dave and I never got over it so we left WV and moved on. We were bitter over it for a long time but it taught me a very valuable lesson about taking full responsibility. Had I been a better up-line they would not have left. You see we are always responsible for the results in our lives and we have nobody to blame for our successes or our failures. That was an expensive lesson. The reps that left our team and joined someone else's team became top earners in the industry. Today I'm thrilled for their success and I'm so impressed with Mike, Dan and Wayne for taking a tiny little company and turning into a huge success. Their choice to bring Marc Accetta in as their head training was the smartest thing they ever did. Marc Accetta's training program is second to none!

The third thing you need to do to pick the right company is find one that is stable, yet still growing. 99% of startups fail. I know from experience. I spent the first 9 years of my Social Marketing career in startups, and while they are exciting, they are also very challenging. As a rule of thumb you should never join a Social Marketing company doing less than $3 million a month, or is less than 3 to 5 years old. In a perfect world you look for a Social Marketing company that is 5 years old, doing over $5 million a month in volume. That way, the company is young enough so that the market is not burnt, and old enough to be out of the danger zone. Startups are exciting and big companies are stable, but the key is to find a company in the middle.

I also believe with today's economy you are wise to find a company that is legitimately open and operational in multiple countries. With the power of social media my team has spread into 12 countries now, but I have only been to 4 of them!

If your company is not international you are missing the boat in a big way. The local economy is becoming a global economy, as the world gets smaller your market gets bigger. It's amazing to watch our industry change with every passing year. The fundamentals will always remain, but right now if you want to hit it BIG in Social Marketing you need to THINK BIG, you need to think global not just local. Local first, but don't build a castle on the sand. If you build a strong team in a company with no global vision, you've really shot yourself in the foot.

Chapter 4
The Basics: Building Your Foundation

Know Yourself

Why are you doing this? What motivates you? What will get you out of bed on a cold and wet Monday morning, when you feel like you were hit by a truck on Sunday? I had one why. It was my Mom. She deserved a better life, a bigger life. She did a lot for my brother and I, just like many single moms; but this was my mom. About a year and a half after our parents divorced, they got remarried, hoping they could make it work, but they couldn't. Things got tough financially and emotionally. My mom was heartbroken, we moved into a small apartment in low-income housing, and I heard my mom cry herself to sleep every night. To make things worse, she had a herniated disk and was constantly in pain. She couldn't stand for too long or sit for too long. Dave and I helped as much as we could with housework, but I'm sure we could have been better at supporting her emotionally. I dove into Social Marketing all the way. Everyone avoids pain in different ways; some go to a bar, while others hit the gym. For me it was work, because I didn't just want to escape, I wanted to climb.

We were getting assistance with food from the church, which really embarrassed me and hurt. I remember telling my mom we didn't need the help and with her eyes full of tears she said, "I'm sorry, Clif, we do." I guess it was then I decided I was going to have to do something, I just didn't know what it was yet. A few months later I ended up in an opportunity meeting and my prayers were answered.

If the Why is Big, the How Becomes Easy

What drives you? What are you passionate about? Is it more time with your kids? Is it to fire your jerk boss? Is it that you love what you do, but could use a little more money? For me it was bettering myself and helping others. I knew my why, now I had my vehicle.

Social Marketing is so cool because you can start part time, with very little money, and you don't need any special background or training. Now that can also be the worst thing about Social Marketing, by the way.

We get all kinds joining; that's for sure.

When you try to help people get in touch with why they are doing this, most will give you a surface answer, but ask them to dig deeper. Why do they want that new car? Get down to their pool of emotion. Emotion moves us, not things. It's not *what* they want, it's *why* they want it that will move them to action.

Know Your Company, Industry, and Product or Services

Industry
- Why is your Industry stable or booming? Support it with facts. Do your research. Understand your industry and how it fits into the local, national and global picture.

Company
- When was the company founded? Who founded it? Why did they start it? Highlight the benefits of your company. You need to know your company's vision for the future and you need to be on board with that.

Products or Services
- What products or services do you provide? Why should people use your products or services? Be able to define and defend the costs. What are the benefits, what are the packages? Where are they made? Why are they better? Remember to follow the 80/20

rule, 80% results and 20% logic. Compare your product or service to a few other brands and show why yours is a better choice. You need to understand the products and why they have value. You don't need to be an expert on the products or services but you have to know the basics. When people ask you crazy details on the products or services here is a coin phrase you can use:

"Well I'm not sure, I'm new, but let me find out and get back to you."

You are not the company. Don't try to be the company. You are a rep. Humor and honesty goes a long way. Here's what I often say when people ask me crazy details on the products:

"I'm not sure, actually I'm on the marketing side. I didn't formulate the product (I say this with a little laugh) Let me find out and get back to you."

Honest. Simple. Straightforward.

Once you realize you don't have to be an expert, you'll relax and so will they. If the person is genuine, they'll usually say "OK, cool". If they are not they will give you crap about not knowing your stuff no matter what your answer is. Don't get stuck becoming a product expert.

Facts Tell and Stories Sell
Think about the last commercial you saw

on TV for shampoo, they are all the same. They give you one or two scientific reasons why their product works, then they instantly go into results, a girl walking down the street or on a date looking fabulous with a smile like she has the secret to beauty!

You want to always keep everything you do 80% emotion to 20% logic. Talk a little about how amazing the product is, but a lot about results and testimonies. Imagine you are selling vitamins and someone asks you why they are the best. Here's an over simplified but accurate way to handle it.

"Well I don't know, I'm an idiot, but all I know is I feel better than I ever felt before and I can work 2 hours longer than I used to."

You get the point. I see so many people that want to build big teams get so caught up in the product that they never build a team. You have to know your product and your company and the founder, but you don't have to become an expert. In fact as soon as you are, then you are no longer duplicatable.

People need to look at you and say, "Wow that looks fun and easy. I could do that!"

Know Your Team
I know…you don't have a team yet. But I'm confident you will, and if you want to

build a team, you've got to understand people. There are dozens of personality theories out there, and if you have time, they're fun to explore, but I like to keep things simple. When you're beginning to build your team, understand there are 4 basic personality types: Controller, Promoter, Analyzer and Supporter, much easier to remember as Sharks, Dolphins, Urchins and Whales!

SHARK	**DOLPHIN**
URCHIN	**WHALE**

SHARKS

- Sharks are money motivated, goal oriented. Driven and focused on results, they are the Controllers. There are good sharks and bad sharks, so don't let the name fool you. Notice the Sharks and Dolphins are on top. This is because they are fast moving. They make decisions quickly. If you talk too slow to them, they will lose interest. Get to the point and be brief. They can't stand long talks. Sharks usually prefer Coke over Pepsi because they like the strong bite of a Coke. Sharks like power colors like red, black, white… maybe a little grey. Mercedes targets these people in their commercials. A Shark's primary motive is power and getting the job done.

WHALES
- Whales are the opposite of the Shark is the Whale. Whales are very caring, they are the Supporters, they love to hug trees, cry at a sunset and probably drive a Prius. Their primary motive is doing good. Subaru targets this market in their commercials. They usually wear earth tones like brown or green, beige or dark brown. Mother Teresa would be an example of a strong Whale. Whales are great to have on your team. They will help make sure nobody is left behind and the team gets everything done. You really need to enroll these people in a cause bigger than making money to get their full participation. The Whale is on the bottom of the chart, the slower half. Do not push Whales, they need time to see how they feel about things and they do not like fast-talking sales people. They sometimes find the Dolphin to be an attention grabber and the Shark to be heartless.

DOLPHINS

- Dolphins are the Promoters. They love a good time and love to party! They can be flaky. They love to wear bright colors and they prefer Pepsi because it's sweet over Coke. They are the ones out on the dance floor, the movers and shakers. They are very spontaneous and fun to be around. They think and move quickly and get annoyed with long talks or lectures. They are likely to drive a Jeep Wrangler or a sports car. They make decisions quickly and can be spoken to directly. Their primary motive is FUN! If you don't keep your business fun for these people, they will quit. A great saying to remember for this group is, "They can get things done, if you keep things fun."

URCHINS
- Urchins are the Analyzers. They want to crunch the numbers, and are always checking their calendars and spreadsheets. Think of an urchin in the ocean with its arms out collecting data, but they are stuck to a rock not going anywhere. They need all the facts before they will make a decision. Dolphins can get really impatient with these people, Sharks too. Urchins can't stand people that over hype or exaggerate. They can't stand people being late or unorganized. An Urchin's primary motive is peace and stability.

Once you understand each personality type, you'll see how they each can uniquely contribute to your business organization. Be careful not to make the mistake of thinking everyone has to be a Shark! This is one of the biggest secrets.

"It takes team work to make the dream work."

As you read about at the beginning of the book, one of the most explosive Social Marketing companies in our industry was 2by2.net. The company started with Dennis and Sophia Wong, brother and sister, Jeff Morgan, my brother, and me. We started with nothing and within the first 2 years we were doing $4 million a month in business. My brother and I had 67,000 reps under us in 8 different legs and were enrolling about 5,000 new members every 30 days. The key to our success was we had very strong people in each category and we all worked together as a team appreciating what each person brought to the table.

You've probably noticed Sharks are located opposite Whales and Dolphins are opposite Urchins. Sharks and Dolphins think and move fast while Urchins and Whales take longer. Undoubtedly you are right now mentally placing yourself into a group or trying to. We are all primarily 1 of these 4 groups, then we have a back up or secondary personality. For example I'm a Shark, Whale. I want to get things done and help as many people as I can along the way. My brother is Dolphin, then an Urchin. He loves to have fun but he really knows his stuff. To become truly self-actualized, you'll learn and adopt the strengths from all 4-personality types.

When you create your first list of people to invite, it's a good idea to identify people's primary personality type. This way when you make your calls, you can make Whale calls back to back or Shark calls back to back, staying in the zone instead of going back and forth. I'll talk more about this when we get to Inviting.

Don't Pre-Judge

I've been in Social Marketing now full time for 17 years and I still can't tell who will be good and who won't. The best 2 people I ever got on my team were 2 people that really struggled in the beginning. One is my brother and business partner, Dave Braun. He couldn't enroll one person for over 3 months. He ended up becoming one of the highest producing people in the industry and a sought after professional, public speaker.

The other was Duke Tubtim, the biggest Urchin I have ever met. After we enrolled him we almost gave him back his money. Now keep in mind he never asked for his money back. He was very intensely focused on his new business, but Dave and I just thought he'd never do well. We were about to tell him he just wasn't cut out for it. We actually felt bad enrolling him. He didn't produce any results for 2 and a half years, and then year 3 with us he got motivated and just started putting people in front of us day after day. He became our number one earner making over $50K a week and is still a top earner to this day.

There are 2 types of leaders; inspirational leaders and organizational leaders. Dave and I were more inspirational leaders, but Duke became an amazing organizational leader, planner and strategic executer, which inspired many! So don't pre-judge. People will surprise you everyday in everyway. Don't limit people based on your view of them.

"If you look at a man the way he is, he becomes worse, if you look at a man the way he could be, then he becomes what he should be." Les Brown

Chapter 5
Get Started!

Looking back on it now, if you would have told me when I started out that I would make millions of dollars, live next door to celebrities, and drive Lamborghinis, I never would have believed it. Things just unfolded. It's like driving in a dense fog, you can only see about 10 feet in front of you at a time.

I wanted to quit and almost did so many times.

I can honestly say out of all the things I have learned… nothing has been more helpful than the Basic Training I got the day after I joined. I have used this Basic Training for over 10 years now and it works year after year.

-"There are no new fundamentals. There may be new ways of applying them, there may be new ways of looking at them, but fundamentals are old." – Jim Rohn

Direction = Energy

Without direction, you'll get somewhere, but it may not be where you want to go. If you don't know what to do, you won't do anything, or you'll waste time doing the wrong things. To create energy, you have to have direction. Ever been to the grocery store without a list? You wander aimlessly through the aisles, not really knowing what you want. You get a sudden craving for Oreo cookies, so you grab some of those. Then you see an attractive person on aisle 6, so you wander over there. Or have you ever been to the gym without a workout plan? Same outcome: a little bench press, maybe calf machine, follow an attractive person, avoid big sweaty person... you get the point. When you're focused, you'll be able to lead your team.

Every Dud Knows a Stud
Rarely do any of us enroll the next superstar; rather they usually show up in our organization somewhere, usually on or under your 3rd level. I have enrolled people that never did much, but they sponsored their sister, who sponsored their boyfriend, who quit, but not until he enrolled his dad

who became one of my top producers. You may enroll a gardener who cuts the grass of a doctor who enrolls and does nothing but enroll his wife, who wants nothing more than a hobby and ends up being your next top leader. The coolest thing about being in Social Marketing for as long as I have full time is that I have so many crazy things happen it's easy for me to have faith. I know as long as I work hard good things will happen. You don't know how or from where they will come, but believe me they will.

"The harder you work, the luckier you get."

List as Many Names as Possible

Most people join and make a list of 10 or 20 people. This cracks me up! If you treat your new business like a hobby, it will pay you like a hobby. If you treat it like a serious business, it will pay you like a serious business. Let me give you the stats. About 1 out of 4 people you present your business to will join. About 1 out of 4 people you invite will show. You will be able to reach about 1 out of 4 people you try to contact. 2 out of 10 people will work. 1 out of 100 on your team will be a strong leader. So if you do the numbers, you need to list a LOT of people. Don't kid yourself. This is not "do nothing and get rich marketing", it's "Network

Marketing" the key word being "Network." How are you going to get in a business that depends on a network and then list 5 names?

You need to have a hot list or top 20 key people that you really want to enroll and then at least 80 more to even give yourself a fair shot at having a strong first 30 days. Don't worry about who will join and who won't. You'll find out soon enough. Lose your fear of rejection and you will enroll people. Carry that fear with you on every call and nobody will join. People absorb energy, they can feel your expectation. Expect them to join, not reject you.

If I gave you $10.00 for every name you could write down in the next 30 minutes, how many names could you write down? I can't tell you how many countless people have given me 10 names until I pulled out this exercise and then the names started flowing. Don't worry about if they will show or not, join or not, just write down names, even if you don't have their numbers. One of my top producers was my old boss at In-N-Out where I worked for a year when I was in high school. I had lost touch with him for years, but I put his name on my list. One day like magic, I bumped into him at an In-N-Out in Mission Viejo. He had been transferred to a new store and I was attending Saddleback Community

College and went for a burger between classes. He said he would come to a meeting and I was excited, then we lost touch again, but I bumped into him at a party and all but enrolled him right there on the spot. He came to a meeting and joined, he became my first monster in Social Marketing.

The people you think will join won't, and the people you think won't, often will. Here's the Memory Jogger I used to make my first list of people to invite.

MEMORY JOGGER

Your Relatives

Mom, Dad, Sister(s) Brother(s)
Niece(s)Nephews(s)
Grandson(s) Granddaughters(s) Grandfather
(s) Grandmother(s) Son(s) Daughter(s)
Mom's Sister(s) Mom's Brother(s) Dad's
Sister(s) Dad's Brother(s) Male Cousin(s)
Female Cousin(s) Favorite Aunt Favorite
Uncle Mother-In-Law Father-In-Law Sister-
In-Law(s) Brother-In-Law(s)

Friends and Acquaintances

Your BFF

Your Other Friend(s)
Next Door Neighbor(s)
Other Neighbor(s)
Mom's friend(s)
Dad's Friend(s)
Son(s) Friend(s)
Daughter(s) Friend(s)
Your Boss
Favorite Co-worker
Other Co-Workers(s)
Your Boss's Boss
Twitter Friend(s)
Facebook Friend(s)
Myspace Friend(s)
Linked-in Friend(s)
Forum Friend(s)
Social Networking Friend(s)
Your Utube Friend(s)
Your Social Marketing Friend(s)
Your BNI Group
Grammar School Friends
High School Friends
College Friends
Chamber of Commerce
Toastmasters.org
Knights of Columbus
Fraternity Friends
Sorority Friends
Your Teacher(s)
Your Christmas Card List
Friends from Church

Spouse's Best Friend
Sent You Christmas Card
Sent You Birthday Card
Who Calls You At Home?

Social Contacts

Who do you play cards with?
Who do you play golf with?
Who do you play tennis with?
Who do you work out with?
Who do you go Bowling with?
Who do you go to concerts with?

Business Contacts

Who Sold You Your House? (Realtor)
Who Sold You Your House? (Old Owner)
Who Sold Your Old House? (Realtor)
Who Bought Your Old House?
Who Gave You a Mortgage?
Who Sold You Home Insurance?
Who Sold You Life Insurance?
Who Sold You Car Insurance?
Who Sold You Health Insurance?
Who Sold You An Annuity?
Who Sold You Your Car?

Inviting
Say Less to More

"When you're new you can't say the right thing to the wrong person and you can't say the wrong thing to the right person."

So don't be afraid to talk to people. I remember jumping out of my new Mercedes-BenzG500 wearing an Armani suit, sporting a $35K white gold Cartier Tank Frances on my wrist, and noticed the guy next to me kind of check out my gear, so I said, "Hi, What's your name?" He told me, we got to talking, and it didn't take longer than two minutes for me to realize this guy could not be less interested. I got back in my car and thought "Maybe I need more diamonds on my watch, or maybe I should have been driving my Lamborghini today," but it's none of that.

When people are looking for an opportunity, they see one. Now that doesn't mean we don't have to work on our approaches, but it does mean that once you have the basics of inviting down you can rest at night knowing that the people that blew you off really were not into it and they may have just saved you a ton of wasted time. Once your team starts to grow you bet your butt there will be people on your team that you wish were way far away!

People generally know if they are interested very quickly and people hate to be pitched or sold, so I have really perfected inviting down to a science. You don't need one hundred ways to invite 4 people; you need 4 ways to invite one hundred people. In the beginning it's important to get your success story going because the people that follow you will usually start at the same level you do and follow your speed.

Don't forget to balance your team with a healthy mix of Sharks, Dolphins, Urchins and Whales. You know your friends better than anyone. With your knowledge of your prospect, with the 4 personality types we have covered, and with this last final tip you should be able to formulate a great approach.

In addition to 4 Personality Types, there are 3 Basic Relationships

People You Look Up To - The best and almost the only way to get these people, is to ask for their advice on your new business. If you know someone who is very successful, chances are you would value their business thoughts. Explain to them that you have recently gotten into a new business and you would appreciate it if they would take a look at it for you and give you their expert advice.

Your Peers - This can be the toughest group.

The key is to not make yourself the issue, but to edify someone else you want them to meet.

People That Look Up to You - This is obviously the easiest group of people to invite. The key with this group is not to say too much. They will come because they look up to you. Don't give them a reason not to come by over pitching.

Be Enthusiastic

Like I said in a previous chapter, the last four letters of the word enthusiasm stand for I Am Sold Myself. If you are sold on what you're talking about, your prospect will be too. One of the most common questions I get is, "What's the best invitation?" Yes, your approach matters and your word choice matters, but nothing matters more than how you feel and how enthusiastic you are about your opportunity. I have seen people fail miserably in great companies then move on to a much less desirable deal they are really excited about and all of the sudden they are sponsor monsters and kicking butt. It's like Matt says, "It's all about your BS, your belief system".

There is an old saying in Social Marketing:
"You will lose 1 out of 10 people for being over excited, but you will lose 9 out

of 10 for being under excited."

Aside from how you come across, your enthusiasm will also dictate how big you make your list, how many people you call, how long you stick around and more. It's at the core of your success or failure. There are other things of course, but they are all affected by your level of enthusiasm. People are not looking to see what you know about your deal, they are looking to see how you feel. Get excited, find something to get excited about, or get into an opportunity that does excite you.

Be Confident

Don't be arrogant. Don't be rude or pushy. That's one of the things that gives our industry a bad name. New people make one of two mistakes. They either are crazy excited and won't shut up about their company, or they are scared and never say a thing about it. The key is to truly be confident in your opportunity. If you are truly confident, you don't need to hammer people daily about it, and you won't be afraid to talk about it either. You will posses a calm energy that attracts people.

You may be reading this saying "Damn! I don't have that and how can I get it?"

The best way is to hang out with

someone that does. Confidence is contagious. These people are out there in your upline somewhere, but you will have to work hard to earn their attention. When I first started in Social Marketing I didn't have this calm energy I'm talking about. I was a nervous, 19 year old, scared and excited. So like Jim Rohn says, "I made up in numbers what I lacked in skill." I talked to as many people as possible and I said as little as possible. I just got people to the meetings. I did well enough to earn the attention of the top people and the more I hung out with them the more confident I became.

People ask me all the time, when did the worm turn for me, or when did I know this was my calling? To tell you the truth, I never had a moment like that. My confidence grew gradually over time. There were no magic moments, just lots of baby steps, lots of little victories. Robyn Williams, the owner of Choice Center, taught me three little baby wins equal momentum and that if you put enough of those in a row you can fly. Les Brown says, "Nobody rises to low expectations." I was lucky to have uplines that really believed more in me than I believed in myself. Following that simple advice, I went from a scared, 19-year-old kid to a confident, 21 year old millionaire in no time.

I was never a leader in school, but I always felt I was different deep inside, I just didn't know how. When I met Dennis Wong and we had long talks about life and I saw that he and I thought the same way about lots of things, that gave me confidence because he was where I wanted to be. But it wasn't all sitting around thinking. I had to put those thoughts into action. When I hit a goal, I gained confidence. The harder I worked, the more deserving I felt. That gave me confidence. The way to build confidence is through accomplishments, start small and work your way up.

Have a Sense of Urgency

Don't be obnoxious, don't bother people, don't over do it, but if you take every excuse people give you and never stand up for the time sensitive nature of your invitation, you will never get anywhere. If you are having trouble expressing a sense of urgency to your prospects, it's because you don't have one, or you do but your image is more important to you than your business. Anyone who ever accomplished anything great risked their ego and pride. Your ego can cost you a fortune.

One of my coaches in Social Marketing, Mr. Alex Alexander, said it best, "Ego is the anesthesia that dulls the pain of stupidity." Drop your ego and we go! An ego is heavy and will slow you down. The sooner you can stop worrying about what others think the sooner you can express a sense of urgency.

If your friend says they can't make the meeting because their favorite show is on what are you going to say? If you say, "Oh, OK, yeah, I totally understand, maybe next week then." what you have said is "My opportunity is not as important as your TV show and if it is, I'm a weak person that can't stand up for what I believe in."

If your friend was drunk out of his mind and walking to his car, would you let him drive home because you were too scared to confront him? People are driving drunk in life and they need strong people to wake them up. I'm not saying pressure people. I'm saying let them know why it's important that they look at this now. There are a million ways to create a sense of urgency. Remember that people are motivated by the fear of loss more than by the hope of gain. So what is at stake? Is there a leader in town leaving soon that you want your friend to meet? Is there a market open now that may not be soon? Timing is everything. Once you get good at communicating a true sense of urgency, you can move mountains.

Keep it Exclusive

"I refuse to join any club that would have me as a member." - Groucho Marx
People want to be a part of something exclusive. If you want people too bad, they don't want you. People will treat your opportunity as you treat it or less, never more. You have to set the standard. People will respect what you respect. This has a lot to do with how valuable you see your opportunity. You will not effectively be able to hold your opportunity high if you don't believe it is. This is why there are no short cuts to success. You must be authentic. It's not about tricks or techniques, it's about authenticity.

People absorb energy, if you believe your opportunity is amazing and if you believe the market timing is now, then it will come across that way. I had a sense of urgency with my friends because I believed what we were doing was amazing and I knew that once it got big my friends would not get to spend time with the upper leadership. They would be trained by the leaders we created and not the head guys. Which is fine, but I explained to them timing is everything and I urged them to take a look now rather than later. This must be done with tact and class. I would say, "Look, no pressure, check us out anytime you like, we are not going anywhere, but the people that make the most money in any company are the people who saw the vision in the early stages. The people at Apple that made the most were the pioneers who saw it being big before it was big.

Rich people understand the power and timing of trends. There are 3 stages to a trend:

Stage 1 Criticism - "Yeah right, music on a disc, what a joke, that's impossible!"

Stage 2 Resistance - "CDs, how ridiculous! All my music is on cassette tapes. I'm not going to repurchase all my music."

Stage 3 Acceptance - Everyone had a CD player and tapes were gone.

Then the cycle repeated itself with MP3 and now all your music is on your phone. It will change again, it always does.

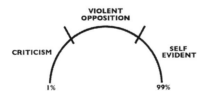

The key is to get in at the beginning when nobody believes. 1% of people stick it out in the beginning and they split 99% of the money. Once it's big and everyone knows about it, you can get a job with the company and you will be one of the 99% splitting up 1% of the money. I was with 3 Social Marketing companies that failed before I was with the one that got me rich. The key is to only join things you really believe in or you will not have the energy it takes to withstand all the criticism and rejection.

It's Not What You Say It's How You Feel About What You Say

We have touched on this a little already, but I'd like to expand this idea. This cannot be faked. Everyone has BS radar. If you don't believe in your words, people will feel it. Remember the UCLA research? Communication is about 55% body language, 38% tone of voice, and only 7% verbal.

I'm not a researcher, but I have been giving presentations and trainings all over the world, and I can tell you that body language and tone reflect your level of certainty in a big way. We could argue percentages all day, but the fact remains that if people are not getting excited about your message the problem lies in your ability to deliver the message. They don't need to buy into you as the expert, remember? Even an idiot knows a few good people. It's not so hard for people to believe that you have bumped into someone worth their time, worth meeting. Don't make yourself the star - edify someone else.

Invite Everyone But Not All at the Same Time

Don't invite more than 4 to 8 guests, because one rotten apple can spoil the whole bunch. There are 5 reasons not to invite too many people at once.

1. You take away the exclusivity and make people feel like a number.

2. You need to have an even number of reps and guests in the room. Too many guests and you will not have any participation. Think of your favorite song, did you sing along the first time you heard it? Of course not, because you didn't know what was coming up next. If you have too many guests in the room and not enough reps everyone is focused on soaking in the information. They are not laughing and clapping a lot, because they don't know where the speaker is headed.

3. If you have an amazing presenter he or she will overcome these obstacles, but now

lets say everyone wants to join except one guy, while you are trying to enroll the first few people he or she is talking others out of it. 2 to 4 guests is ideal.

4. Let's say they all join. They will argue about who goes under who!

5. It's also not easy to train and support 8 new frontline people at the same time. When you enroll people you need to spend time with them. I'm not saying go slow, I'm just saying don't get over excited.

Meeting Conduct

Meeting conduct is one of the most important tools, and it's so rarely done well. I've seen so many bad meetings. Jim Rohn says, "It's just a half dozen things that make 80% of the difference. Every presenter needs to have 2 presentations up his or her sleeve. One is an informal presentation and the other is a formal presentation. You need to know when to use each.

There is nothing worse than having a formal meeting set up with a hotel and a projector, for only 5 people. And you don't want to have just a whiteboard and a marker for a 200 person meeting. Small home meetings need only a few things. First, have some credibility brochures or handouts for your guests. Second, have a TV or laptop on which to play your company video.

Third, unplug the home phone! Fourth, have a few refreshments, drinks and snacks but nothing too fancy or it's not duplicatable. Fifth, have applications on hand ready for the guests. And last but not least, be sure to have reps in the room participating at a normal level, not too much to scare people and not too little so it feels like nobody is into it.

For a formal hotel meeting people should be dressed business casual, no shorts. The meeting should start on time. I don't use a laptop and a projector for home meetings, but I do use them in hotel meetings. I don't do hotel meetings unless we have at least 50 people, preferably 100 to make it cost effective. I don't like charging people at the door. It's awkward. I pay for the meetings myself until I get a few leaders making money, then I have them chip in and eventually take over the cost. You need a projector, a laptop, and music. A laptop and home speakers will work for your smaller meetings, but if your meetings get to be over 100 people you will need to get some more professional equipment.

I always have walk-in music with a slide show so the guests are not asking the reps to give them a presentation before the presentation. I have a slide show playing that gives the reps and guests things to talk about: pictures of the products, pictures of lifestyle results, cars, homes, vacations, etc. Remember we are selling lifestyle after all. Keep the music upbeat, nothing too crazy, but nothing that will put your guests to sleep.

Call me a perfectionist, but one thing I can't stand is when the picture from the projector doesn't match the screen, it looks unprofessional. Get there early, at least one hour early, to make sure you have everything set up properly. Give yourself time to do a sound check, make sure the microphone works, and the laptop presentation is ready. Get there early enough to get the AC going and realize that the room will warm up once you get 50 or more bodies in there, so set it at 60 or 65. Train your reps to sit up, take notes and look alive. Train them to participate, but not to overdo it or make it look cultish.

I like to keep everyone assembled in the hallway until 10 minutes before we start so there is a rush of energy when everyone crowds in. Make sure you have fewer chairs set out than the number of people you are expecting. Nothing looks worse than a bunch of empty chairs in the back. It's always better to have to go get more chairs than take away chairs. Designate certain people to take care of certain things so you

are not running around trying to do it all
yourself.

Early is On Time, On Time is Late, and Late is Unheard Of

Whether you are the new rep bringing
your guest or whether you are the presenter,
being on time is crucial. Being late speaks
volumes about your level of commitment.
Everything you do is being judged,
consciously or unconsciously, by your
guests and your team.

"The pack will only run as fast as the
lead dog."

Get to the meeting 20 minutes early so
your guest can meet other reps in the
company. Introduce them to people like
them, so they can better see themselves
being involved. Even when I didn't have
guests I would go to the meetings to meet
the other reps. I wanted to meet as many
people as I could, so if I had a guest who
was a doctor, I could introduce him to
another doctor who was a rep. If I had a
college student guest I would introduce him
to other college students like him or her.

"If you have a guest the meeting needs
you, if you don't have a guest you need the
meeting."

There were many nights my guests flaked on
me, but I stayed for the meeting because I

knew I needed to get pumped up. Also I wanted to learn how to do the meetings myself, so I would stay and take notes on the speakers.

Pick Up Your Guest

"You don't win by making sensational plays; you win by not making mistakes." - Oail Andrew "Bum" Phillips (NFL Coach 1967-85)

If your guests say they will meet you at the meeting, offer to pick them up, unless it's a stranger. If you meet them there, there is a 60% chance they won't show up. Plus the drive there together and home is important. It's the little things that show you are serious. The time there allows you to *Pre-Talk your guests*, get them thinking about their life, ask them questions like, "What would you do if you had a million dollars right now?" I like this question for two reasons; it gets them to start thinking bigger and allows for them to get excited. Their answer then reveals their personality: Controller (Shark), Supporter (Whale), Analyzer (Urchin) or Promoter (Dolphin). If they say they would invest it, they are an Analyzer and I now know how to work with them. If they say they would take a vacation, chances are they are a Promoter. If they say they would open a business with it, they
96

may be a Shark. If they say they would donate half to a charity they may be a Supporter. You can learn so much about a person with this single question. You always want to know what a person's motives are before the meeting starts and what their personality is.

If I know what someone wants, I can almost always enroll them. A Social Marketing opportunity is so many different things to so many different people. For one person it's an opportunity to work less and spend more time with their kids. For another person it's all about having nicer things. I know lots of people who joined just to have something to do or to accomplish something outside their family business. Some people join because they want to be a part of something bigger than themselves. The key is to find out what makes your prospect tick. Don't sell them *your* dream; *their* dream is what's important. What motivates you may not motivate them.

The Ride Home
The ride home is equally important. It gives you time to answer any questions they may still have, I have had many guests say they have to think about it and not join at the hotel, but then once we got in the car and they didn't feel obligated to join or any

pressure, they opened up on the ride home. The best time to enroll someone is there at the meeting but the car ride home gives you a second chance. Don't badger your prospect the whole ride home, be cool but ask a few questions. We'll talk more about this in 'Opening'.

Introduce Your Guest to as Many People as Possible

We talked about this earlier, so I won't spend too much time on it. The key is to make your guest feel welcome and comfortable. If you introduce them to a lot of people they will feel a part of the program and not like an outsider.

Dress for Success

You don't need to wear a suit and tie to every meeting unless that's the culture your company has developed. I have been in companies where we all suited up for every meeting and it worked and I have been in companies where business casual was the rule and that has worked. The key is to look good. Take pride in yourself and show you care.

Take Notes

If you take notes your guest will take

notes. If they take notes they are paying attention. Monkey see, monkey do. I like to get my guest a water bottle or a glass of water before the meeting. Do you know why this has been done for decades? It's not because we think your guest is thirsty, this technique was developed so that guests could not cross their arms in the meeting. Have you ever tried to cross your arms holding a glass of water? Bring a note pad for your guest and an application.

Leave Your Problems at Home

We all have bad days but we don't all let them control our days. The meeting place is a happy place, a serious place, a place where we are creating an atmosphere of progress. It's not a place for you to show up depressed or bummed out.

"Learn to control your emotions so they serve you, not limit you." Jim Rohn

I can honestly say some of my best presentations ever were my worst days ever. Days where I learned my girlfriend was cheating on me. Days where I learned my top rep left to another company. Days where I found out my car was repossessed. I took that negative energy and turned it into fuel, knowing that feeling sorry for myself was not the answer. You can cry when you get home. If you bring a bad attitude to a meeting you are letting down not only yourself and your team, but you are killing the opportunity for your guest to get the full experience.

You need to learn to think of others, not just yourself. We all have problems but we all have a choice on how we can respond to them. Two pieces of advice here, change your life so you have less problems and change your attitude on how you handle them. You have to get tougher. I have given presentations right after being chewed out by my sponsor or by the owner of the company. I gave a presentation knowing there was a guy outside waiting to fight me and I did great. I did a presentation while my ex girlfriend sat in the front row with her new boyfriend just to try to throw me off. I could go on and on but it comes down to this: How bad do you want it? Grow up; get tougher and stop feeling sorry for yourself. Every successful person has a story you don't know about. However hard you think it was for them, it was probably harder.

Don't Ask Your Upline For Help With Anything in Front of Your Guest at a Meeting

I don't know why they call it common

sense; it's not common at all. I've had reps walk up to me after an amazing meeting, everyone is fired up and their guest looks excited too. Then they throw up all over me with a story on how hard it is to recruit people. The first time this happened to me I was stunned, I looked at their guest's face and saw the enthusiasm fade to fear in a blink of an eye. It's OK to have challenges in the business, we've all had and currently have them, but the presentation is not the place to air these issues. Again, it all has to do with your focus. Are you thinking of yourself or your prospect? If your focus was truly on helping your prospect, then you would not be asking for help in front of them. The focus would be on them. "If you help enough people get what they want you can have everything you want." Jim Rohn

Participate

Smile, nod, and clap, but don't be a freak. I know I said it's better to be over excited than unenthusiastic. It's true if you don't show it, people won't know it, but if you fake enthusiasm and use it as a technique, it will turn people off. Mindless zombies over participating really take away from the validity of the opportunity. I've seen really good presenters have people in the audience over participate and kill it for the guests. Here is how you would participate correctly. If the room's energy is at a 3, chime in at a 4. If the room's energy is at a 6, chime in at a 7. Slowly, naturally bring up the energy. Nodding your head is OK, taking notes is OK. Yelling out and being weird throws off the speaker and freaks people out.

There are 2 types of people in a meeting. Givers and takers, people that give energy to the meeting and people that suck it out from the meeting. The proper way to give energy to a meeting is to smile warmly into the speaker's eyes, lean forward, and look alive! The way to suck energy from the meeting is to have poor posture, lean back, fold your arms, or text while the speaker is talking. I have actually seen people fall asleep! The speaker is half responsible for the meeting and the audience is half responsible for the energy in the meeting.

It's better to have an OK speaker and a genuinely excited audience than a great speaker with a dead or over hyped audience. If the speaker is amazing and the audience is too scared to participate or over participating the guests says to themselves this is going to be too hard for me or this is weird. If you don't know what is too much or too little, watch a meeting by a company in real momentum and you feel the energy.

Opening vs. Closing

I call it opening because it's not closing at all! We are not in sales, we are in marketing and there is a big difference. When you sell a car you close the deal. When you ink a contract, you close the deal. In our business when you enroll someone you are starting something, not ending it. You are helping them open their own small business. Plus thinking of it this way helps you to realize that your job is just starting.

You should have been reading your guests reactions the whole time. Were they into it? Were they nodding? Were their arms crossed? It's very important to read body language during the meeting. Body language never lies, people do. If they tell you it was great but they have to go think about it, look back to their body language. Were they tapping their feet? Were they holding their keys? Were their feet pointed towards the door? Were their arms and legs crossed? Were they not taking notes? If these are true they are totally not into it.

The better the presentation the less "closing" you have to do.

Great Presentation = Less "Closing"

Bad Presentation = Lots of "Closing"

Remember the 4 fish. (Yes, I know that zoologically speaking this is not technically correct, only the shark is a fish, but it's easier to remember!)

When opening your guest, you can push a Shark or Dolphin a little, but not a Whale or Urchin, they are slower and they need more time to think about the numbers or how they feel about everything. If you push them you will lose them. Use the technique "match and mirror." Some people talk fast and you have to communicate quickly to them, some people talk very slow and you need to talk slow when talking to them. Sometimes I realize I'm so unlike the prospect I'll have one of my reps who is more like them come talk to them for me.

There are some key phrases to use when opening that work very well but aren't pushy or too direct like, "So do you see a way to make money here?" Or even better if you pre-talked them before the meeting and found out what their hot buttons are you can be more specific. For example, if your prospect told you they would like to spend more time with their kids you may ask them at the end of the meeting, "So do you see this as a way to spend more time with your kids?" You get the picture.

Sometimes you can't get a read on your
104

guest. If this is the case don't be afraid to ask them what they are thinking. Here's an example of what I say.

"Ben, you look like you're thinking about something, what is it?"
Or sometimes you can tell they want to join but they are hesitant. Then I will say, "Ben I can see you are interested but it looks like there is something holding you back."

The key is to remember to be human. Have a conversation, care about the person, and remember they are a person not just a prospect. The more they feel that you really care about them and you are not just in a hurry to sign them, the more they will open up to you. Matt Morrow, Social Marketing expert and long time friend of mine, always says, "People don't care how much you know until they know how much you care."

A few years ago, Matt and I were driving in his RV home back to California from Las Vegas after a Convention where he and I spoke on stage for maybe 3,000 people at the MGM Grand. We like to think that we were the best speakers that day, and I really think we were, but we were both unhappy about the event because our team was not winning the most awards and we both knew why. Sometimes when you have been doing Social Marketing for so long, it's easy to let things become too rote, and to almost fall out of touch with the basics.

Matt made a turn off the highway and we drove to meet a woman that changed Matt's life many years ago. Her name was Robyn Williams and she's a guru, the closest thing to Yoda you will ever find. She looks nothing like Yoda, but you know what I mean. Matt registered me for a $3,000.00 class where I learned about the power of enrollment. When you sign people up it's all about you. When you enroll people you are getting them on board with you by their own free will. It takes more energy, it takes you opening up and connecting, being vulnerable and authentic. It was the best course I have ever taken. I'll never forget the people I met or the experiences I had. The course was called Choice Center and I highly recommend it for anyone. I met the vice president of Coca Cola, a real-estate multimillionaire, moms, construction workers, and teachers - you name it. The range of people who participated in the course was far and wide.

Up until that time, because I had spoken on stage for thousands of people, I considered myself an expert on personal development, but this course blew me away. Once you really learn to harness the power of enrollment your whole life will explode into change.

The Fortune is in the Follow-up

You will notice charismatic people are great at starting up conversations and creating interest, but are often lousy at follow up. Organized, conservative people are great at follow up. This is why it's great to have a partner or friend you can work with to balance things out. If you look at almost every great Network Marketing success, they all had a partner, not an actual partner on their position, but someone they worked closely with in their downline that was good at what they were not.

If you can't enroll them on the spot, you have 48 hours to get them back to another meeting. Why 48 hours? Because their life will take over, their emotion will drop and they will forget about it. Here's a chart to help you understand.

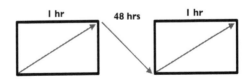

You want everyone singing the same song or people take too much time making their own manuals, avoid making their own calls. It's all about how they spend their time. I've seen it time and time again, if you don't have a manual that's the bible of your dang deal, you can bet your butt some genius will make one, and it probably won't be a good one.

Then someone will see his or her manual and says, "Wow, those graphics look like stock images from Word 2000, I can do better than that!" So they spend their first month creating a manual with the best images, but the content is way off, and so the next person produces their manual and now you have a small group of people making manuals and the rest of your team divided spending time debating over which manual is the best and should be the official team manual. They will never agree, so they will separate into different groups and it all falls apart. Don't waste your time reinventing the wheel.

One Team, One Dream, One Damn Manual!

The manual is important but anyone who has made $20K a month or more can make a decent manual. The key is everyone follows it so your team is on the same page in every city and every state. It shows new people you guys know what you are doing, you have a system, and it's working

Chapter 6
Stay Focused: Personal Development

If it wasn't for Social Marketing I don't think I would have ever discovered the power of personal development, at least not fully. Many people in life excel without listening to the audio files or reading the books, but they may be in industries where teaching and duplication is not as crucial as it is in our business. So while your friend in the music business or on Wall Street may be successful without listening to a lot of personal development tapes, remember that training and duplication is not the key component to their business, while it is in ours. At the same time, you would be surprised at how many successful people in entertainment are really big on personal development. It's important in any business, but it's at the core of ours.

Not only do you need to keep yourself motivated, you need to motivate your team and eventually, teams. Anthony Robbins talks about having an hour of power everyday. He recommends you listen to or read something positive daily. As I look back at my 17 years in Social Marketing, I can see very clearly the years I was really heavy into personal development were, without exception, my biggest moneymaking years. I can remember the first time my sponsor turned me on to Jim Rohn, I was like "Wow, this is lame!" Then about 10 minutes into it I was like, "Wow, this is amazing stuff!"

I was really lucky to have been introduced to Jim Rohn at 19. As we get older we tend to get more cynical and obtuse. At 19, I soaked it all up. Jim Rohn made everything seem so simple; I couldn't believe everyone didn't listen to him and implement his philosophies. Jim Rohn put me light years ahead of most people my age, and he, or someone like him, can do the same for you.

As I said in Chapter 1, I tried hard to get my team to listen to Jim Rohn, but out of every 10 people I would recommend him to, maybe one person would go out and buy his book or CD and listen. So eventually my brother and I discovered it was better for us to listen to inspirational speakers, internalize their wisdom, and then incorporate it into our presentations and trainings.

Of course, Jim Rohn wasn't my only

source of inspiration. He simply expressed basic truths in a way that got through to my 19-year-old self. I continue to admire his writing, listen to many speakers, and keep an open mind. I keep my ears open, too. I never know when I will learn something that will help me in my business and my life, whether it's from a waiter or a CEO. Think of truth as a large diamond that was shattered; pieces of the truth are scattered all around us. We just need to recognize them when we find them, whether it's in a Jim Rohn talk, a book by the Dalai Lama, one of your grandfather's stories, or a complete stranger you sit next to on a plane.

Personal development is such a big part of my life. By 27, my brother and I had made millions and surpassed many of our goals. Money poured in daily. When you are in your twenties and making over $3,000.00 a day, it's hard not to get a little ego.

I would say it was around 27 or 28 that we stopped listening to personal development and became "experts". But the funny thing about personal development is it's not a destination, it's a lifelong habit. It's like a shower; you don't shower once, get clean and then stop taking showers. It didn't happen overnight, but slowly things started to slow down and we realized why. Personal development is a must in our business and hanging around charactered, positive people is a must. Jim Rohn always says, "Influence is two things, powerful and subtle."

The best program to start out on is "Challenge to Succeed." by Jim Rohn. We have heard all his programs and read all his books. We have had dinner with him, been to his seminars and even talked to him on the phone imitating his voice which he got a real kick out of. Jim has a very unique accent that you love or hate. Luckily for him and us, most people love it. Unfortunately, Mr. Rohn has passed away, but he has left us with a wealth of knowledge.

Maybe it's just because I heard Jim first or maybe it's because I like his style, but he always has been my favorite and he always will be. I still watch his videos on YouTube and listen to his audio programs. I think it's important to listen to a wide variety of speakers and here is why. At 19 there was a lot of Jim Rohn I could incorporate into my presentations and trainings because it was all deep yet simple. However it's only natural that you start to talk a little like the person you listen to most and being 19 but talking like you are 60 can be weird at times! LOL!

I then moved on to Les Brown, whom I liked because he gets you fired up, then Zig Ziglar, who has more techniques and religious references than anyone in the business. Then Stephen Covey, Brian Tracy, Bill Baily, Jerry Ballah, Larry Huff, Anthony Robbins, John Milton Fogg, Rand Gage, Mark Hughes, and more.

I have spent thousands on audio programs and seminars. I believe to this day the best trainer in our industry was Mr. Bill Gouldd. Some don't think he's a nice guy, and if you watch his videos on YouTube he comes across as an egomaniac, but the one thing he had was certainty. If you lack confidence you can watch his videos and borrow his, he has enough for an army! Be careful listening to Bill Gouldd, if you listen too much you can become very hard to be around. People love him or hate him. A lot of great motivational speakers and trainers came from Bill....Dani Johnson, Marc Accetta and more.

Again, it's important to listen to as many people as possible because you need to find someone you can imitate for a while until you develop your own style. I would say I'm most like Mark Hughes mixed with a lot of Jim Rohn and a little Bill Gouldd at times with some Robert Downey, Jr. Yeah, I'm weird, but hey, it worked for me. You have to find your own style. If you stick with it and listen to enough people you will develop your own genuine style.

One of the benefits to listening to personal development is it helps you never be at a loss for words. If a rep has a problem, I have at least three answers for them. This comes from experience and from being a good student. Jeff Olsen wrote a great book called "The Slight Edge" and in this book he talks about how it's the little things we do or don't do that add up over time. Jim Rohn says success and failure are not catastrophic events. They are built over time. You fail or succeed based on thousands of little decisions made daily over a few years. You don't gain weight overnight; your relationship doesn't go from perfect to awful overnight.

Failing takes time.

Success takes time.

In a way we really all do get what we deserve. Now bad things may happen to you, but bad things happen to everyone.

On the surface you may look at someone else's life and say, "Wow, they seem to have it made." But what you don't see is all the bad things that happened and how they responded to these events in a mature way with a positive attitude. This is why personal development is so important. Bad things happen to all of us, but it's how we respond that counts.

If you are not "in the zone" and

something bad happens, you may be too tired or too depressed to tackle it the right way. For example, let's say you haven't been working out lately, you haven't been reading positive books, and your relationships are not at their peak right now. On top of that you get yelled at by your boss.

Chances are if you are tired, down, and out of shape when those things happen, and maybe even a tad hung-over from staying out the night before drinking, you will *react* instead of respond and your reaction will be one you will regret later.

If you can learn to *respond* instead of react, you will be much better off. By consistently seeking out opportunities for personal development, you'll be full of energy; hope and vitality, prepared to respond instead of react mindlessly to challenges in your life.

Reaction or Response

There is a split second between when an event occurs and we decide to either react or respond. It's there that our character comes into play.

In his book, "*Man's Search for Meaning*", Victor Frankl talks about making this very choice. During his time in a concentration camp, he saw many people killed right in front of him. His wife, brother, mother, and father, were all murdered or died in the camps. He had every right to hate the Nazis, but he realized he had a choice. He could either hate (reaction) or love (respond). He obviously chose love and through his work and writings he has helped many others to do the same.

The underlying character you develop greatly affects whether you react without thinking, or respond positively. You can try to fool others that you have it together and that you are on track, but you can't fake character. It will be revealed by your actions.

Have you ever heard the saying, "Time will either promote you or expose you"?

This is true because your character determines your actions and over time they become very visible to everyone. The toughest part is they usually become very visible to everyone but you. It's always easier to see others' flaws rather than our own.

Feedback

A huge part of personal development is feedback. I'm not talking about people yelling at you or people putting you down. I'm talking about people that really care about you and they are trying to give you constructive criticism in an effort to help you move forward better. The sooner you can learn to accept feedback and grow from it, the closer you will be to achieving your goals. If one person tells you you're being an ass, so what? If 2 people tell you, maybe they both don't like you. But if 3 or 4 or 5 people tell you you're an ass you better get a saddle!

Feedback, oh feedback, we hate it! We all hate it but we all need it. What we need to hear is usually what we don't want to hear. If you want to make it BIG in Social Marketing you will have to learn to accept feedback without getting down on yourself.

1. You need to be around the right kind of people that care about you enough to give you feedback.

2. You need to learn to accept it.

3. You need to learn to pick yourself back up and move on!

I have seen so many people have the right friends, get the right feedback, see what they never saw before and really get it.

But then they are so down on themselves they can't move forward. My good friend Danny Bae and I were in Korea recently and he said something great. He said, "The best part of realizing you're the problem is knowing that you are also the solution!" If you are the problem you can fix it! The worst is when it's not you. Then what do you do? Changing ourselves is easy. Trying to change others is a waste of energy.

"If You Want More You Must Become More."

This is the core of Jim Rohn's philosophy and should become the corner stone for your new business. No matter what business you are in you have to deal with someone, often times many people. The better you are with relationships, the more successful your business will be. Tony Robbins talks about how relationships can make your life heaven or hell. In Napoleon Hill's book, "*Think and Grow Rich*", he names 10 things you need to get rich, and at the top of the list is 'harmony in human relationships'.

The best gift you can give anyone is a better you. If you become more, you strengthen every aspect of your relationships and you will attract new and better relationships to you. If you are a 7 in organization it will be hard for you to attract, let alone lead someone who is 9 in organization. If you are a 3 as a leader, you will not be able to attract an 8 as a leader into your business. We always talk about recruit up and yes we want you to do that, but that doesn't mean don't work on yourself at the same time! If you're an overall 7 you may recruit an overall 8 but you won't be able to consistently attract and lead 9's.

Still not convinced personal development is the key to success in Social Marketing? Then think about this:

"If you could have everything you wanted by being who you are, you would already have it." - Clif Braun

We all need to move forward. Even if you are at a high level, you still need to focus on personal development because we are always going up or down, never still. As a body builder gets bigger and bigger it gets harder and harder for him or her to gain muscle mass, they have to spend more time in the gym for smaller gains. When you first start reading personal development books you will grow by leaps and bounds, but as you move on you will find it harder and harder to make these huge leaps. You may read a whole book on a certain topic and only learn a few new things but the very act of reading the book keeps you in the zone and walking the walk you're talking. Once you are ripe, you rot. Always stay green. Once you become a know-it-all, nobody will like you. For starters, no one will follow you and you will lose the current team you have. It's like a cancer.

Trust me…. I know … I had it! Luckily, I had good people around me that pointed it out. I saw it, realized it, and worked on it. The key is to identify the problem and then focus on the solution. Don't dwell on it. Everyone loves a comeback story.

Character is not like a nice suit you can just put on when you want to look good, and it can't be changed over night. I forget which Star Wars it is, but Anakin Skywalker decides to go the dark side to learn how to save his bride, because the Sith Lord says he can teach him how to bring back the dead. The Sith Lord says for Anakin to kill a bunch people, even kids, so the darkness can grow in him before he is ready to really discover the powers of the dark side. Well, it's kind of like that. You can't be really bad or really good overnight.

You have to work at it, that may not be the best example, but you get the point. Character is built and lost over time, not in a seminar or after reading one book. You really have to work at it. If you want to develop character and grow and develop as a person the first thing you need to do is hang around the right people and limit your relationships with the wrong people.

There are some people you should not be around at all. So look at your life and figure out who is who. If someone is always putting you down that may be a toxic relationship from which you need to separate yourself. If someone parties too much and is fun to hang out with, that may be someone you can visit once a month, but maybe not every day. Then there are those you want to spend *more* time with, the people that inspire you and motivate you, the people that want what's best for you.

My definition of a friend comes from Jerry Ballah, who said a friend is a person who wants success for you as bad as you do. I've only known a few people like this in my lifetime. But they have been huge impacts on my life. They're out there; they may be living with you. We all have them in our life or nearby; we just might not recognize them all the time.

Which brings me to my next point, who

are you being daily? Are you the type of person people want to help? You have to earn the attention of the right people. They are busy and they don't spend time with people that are perpetually needy, but rather with people that deserve it. So ask yourself, do you deserve the help and attention of the people you want to be around? If not, change.

The greatest thing about Social Marketing is that our uplines, for the most part, really are motivated to help us. If you show a little effort, they will notice. If you produce some results, they will notice. But you have to step up first. Everyone says, "I'm your next top guy!" but you have to show them you're the one.

Everyone gets their personal development in different ways, some people like to read it, some people like to hear it in audio, and some people love going to seminars. The how is not important. What matters is that you get the information in your head and you apply it in your life.

The best way to remember what you have learned is to share it with others. Take what you have learned and use it, share it, live it. Don't just let the information go from the speaker or the book to your head. You have to breathe life into the information by using it. There are so many people that read the books and go to the seminars, but never make any progress. I call them the "warm and fuzzy people." They just like to get the "warm and fuzzies." They are the people that feel like learning will get them somewhere, but we all know knowledge is only potential power. All the knowledge in the world won't help a person who won't take action.

What's stopping these people is fear. The less they do, the more they think. The more they think, the more they fear…and the less they do. It's a vicious cycle. It's like fat people eating because they are unhappy and then getting fatter and becoming unhappy. Like a drug addict escaping their problems with drugs, then their problems get worse, so they do more drugs.

The warm and fuzzy people I'm talking about are the people who are addicted to affirmations and new beginnings, but never take a step. Yes, we tell you to go the seminar or meeting, but that alone won't take you where you want to go. What if you went to every meeting and never brought a guest? Would that work? Of course not, so it's important to realize that you can't just watch the movie, The Secret, all day and imagine checks getting slid under your door.

In the Bible, God talks about how we have to do our part. I'm not going to get religious here, but I'm just saying I've read the book three times and there is some really good stuff in there! Jim Rohn says labor is the miracle part. Nothing happens without it. So how do you know if you're one of the warm and fuzzy people? You already know!

If you haven't enrolled a new member in 6 months or more, but you have been to 3 or more seminars or read 3 or more books or CD's or whatever, you are a warm and fuzzy person and this is your intervention! STOP! Start DOING something! Action is the only thing that will stop your fears. Stop planning, stop living in the past or in the future, and do something today.

Do one positive thing every day that you hate doing! Not the warm, fuzzy crap you love to do every day to avoid doing the real stuff. Identify and get in touch with IPA What's IPA? Income Producing Activities

Not Facebook.

Not organizing your desk.

Not watching *The Secret* again for the thousandth time.

Not doing laundry or rearranging the furniture.

Income Producing Activities are getting

in front of people and talking about your business. Now let me make a disclaimer. Cleaning your office and watching The Secret are all great and they can be a launch pad for you to jump into the real work, but just remember that if you spend more time cleaning, thinking and organizing than you do presenting, training or recruiting, you are only fooling yourself. Can Facebook be a business-building tool? Sure! But make sure you spend 80% of your time recruiting, 19% of your time training, and 1% of your time problem solving.

So what percent do I dedicate to Facebook? 0%! If your 80% of recruiting time has a little Facebook in there, that's OK. If your 20% of training time has some Facebook in there, that's OK. But sitting on Facebook putting out motivational quotes all day long is not really recruiting. Trust me I know, it can be addicting! I've been there. I'm guilty of it too! We love the connection we get from people and that's OK, but don't fool yourself. I'll cover the social media stuff later, there is a use for it, but it must be monitored carefully.

Chapter 7
Energy

What Energy Do You Bring To the Table?

Life is energy. This business is energy. You may have heard the saying, "People will be more impressed with the height of your enthusiasm than the depth of your knowledge."

This is not true for your doctor or your attorney. When you hire them you are looking for their level of expertise, but the saying holds true in our business 100%. It also holds true for most things in our lives. We are emotional beings; we make our decisions based 80% on emotion and 20% on logic. Don't believe me? Look at who you are married to or who you are dating. Was that a logical, thought out decision or was it based on your feelings?

You can't fake energy, people see right through it. They may not see the real you, but they will see that you are not the you,

you claim to be. If you want people to follow you in this business you must develop and create the right energy. If you stay up late and party all night, when you meet with your team's prospects the next day you will be tired, hung over, and slow. If you continue this long enough you can add feelings of shame and guilt to your tiredness. I know, I've been there!

Once my team was huge and I was making over $100K a month I felt I had earned the right to party a little. The thing is when you don't run out of money and you don't have to go to work the next day, it's easy to let the party carry on and on and on…

Maybe partying is not your problem; maybe it's self-doubt. If you are talking to your prospects and you doubt yourself, your product, or your company - even your upline, it will show through. When you believe in yourself, your product, and your company, it shows. I would rather have one new, excited guy with true belief than 20 has-been, know-it-all, jaded leaders. Nothing beats coachable enthusiasm and passion. Now if you have been in Social Marketing for a while and you bought this book because you are down and out and you read this and say "Oh no I'm screwed! I'm a jaded, broke, know-it-all, has-been leader!"

Stay calm. I have been there.

I got out of it, and you can too. I was listening to a Tony Robbins CD yesterday and he was talking about how one of the first things race car drivers get taught is how to come out of a spin, how to regain control once they have spun wildly out of control. He said the first thing you must do is stay calm and focus on where you want to go. It's the same for us. Life is so cyclical, if you are up now, a down time is coming and that's OK. If you are down now, an up time is coming - so get ready! Remember ...the only thing constant is change.

You Deserve Success

The key to getting your energy in place is feeling like you deserve success. If you want it and work towards it, but don't feel you deserve it, you don't have the edge. Everyone wants to do better, but not everyone feels they deserve it. Once you feel you deserve it, your posture changes, you look people in the eyes and people respond differently to you. This is what you want, this is what you need, that certainty and clarity. I have heard it called blue energy. An energy that is calm and confident, not a fake, hyped-up energy where you are really trying to convince yourself, but a real, true-blue energy that helps you move like water, taking the path of least resistance, smart energy that gets you where you want to go without force.

Sounds great, right? So you're probably asking yourself how do I get this energy? The way you get this energy is by earning it. Jim Rohn says character is not like cologne that you can spray on when you want to smell good. It's also not something you are born with and cannot change. It's something we must all work on, one day at a time.

You Are Who You Are, Not What You Say

It's funny how we all say the same stuff in different ways. I always said, "It's not what you say, it's who you are." Darren Hardy says, "It's not the words, it's the person behind the words." And I could tell you how 8 other guys said the same thing, but in different ways. The point is these are fundamentals that never change.

People always ask me, "Clif, how can I recruit better? What should I say?"

I don't mean to poke fun at these people, but I do laugh a little when people ask me these questions because what you say is not nearly as important as who you are. I was at Wesley Snipes' birthday party in the Hollywood Hills and I saw the actor Billy Zane say to a girl, "Where have you been all

130

my life?" She was swept off her feet and they started chatting and later I believe left the party together. If some average guy said the same thing to that pretty girl she would have laughed and made fun of him later to her friends for using such an old, corny pick-up line. It's not the words; it's the person behind the words. Billy Zane is super cool, rich and good looking. He is ambitious and talented. She saw that and said in her head, "Wow this guy is cool and special."

No, you might not be rich or great looking and famous, but you don't need to be. If you believe in what you are saying and if you are enthusiastic, if you are really working hard towards accomplishing your goals and being a better person, if you really care about your prospect and want to work with them towards a goal that serves both of you and helps other people at the same time, people will listen.

People Don't Join Your Company, They Join You

If you want people to join you and follow you then you must work on yourself. People don't join your company; they join you. So it's not what you are saying or what you are doing that is wrong, it's worse. It's who you are.

Now don't shoot the messenger; I'm just

being real. If people are not joining your team, there's a reason and it's you every time. But how cool is that? If it's you, then you can change it! If you were a victim of something else you would be powerless and unmotivated, wouldn't you? If you feel powerless and unmotivated it's because you are lost or you feel like a victim. Once you realize that you are the problem you should feel empowered. This is a great thing; now you can change.

When I first got to South Africa there was no team here. There were a few reps that were very down and de-motivated. One of them was talking to me about Vemma and you could tell he was very down, even though he was saying all the right stuff about how they must just carry on and focus on the positive, etc. You could see he didn't believe anything he was saying. I have been here for almost a year now and business is now booming, we have 30-40 people a day joining and the energy is off the charts, not because I'm some superman, but because I have learned how to empower people to be their best.

Anyway I was just chatting to that same guy, I heard he got a new girlfriend, I asked him about her and right away a huge smile came over his face, he turned and looked at me and said, "Clif, I'm happy. I'm really,

really happy." He didn't say anything magical, his words were simple, "I'm happy." People ask me all the time how it is that I personally enroll 2-3 people a week and make it look effortless.

I said, "It is effortless. I work out everyday, I eat healthy, I take care of myself, I'm friendly to everyone I meet. I tell jokes that make people laugh and I care about people. I don't try to recruit anyone. I make friends with people and that's it."

The second they feel you are trying to recruit them and you have not developed any rapport with them you are dead in the water. Before you ask for their hand you must touch their heart.

Now you might be saying, "Well, shoot, Clif, I got bills to pay! I don't have time to win everyone over and touch their hearts." You can touch someone's heart in less than a minute. If you get yourself together and live a good life people will see it on your face right away. Go to the gym, eat healthy, and listen to Tony Robbins. It's not that hard to figure out. There are no shortcuts in life.

I think Tony Robbins said, "Remember that your brain is the most powerful computer in the world, but it doesn't come with an owner's manual and it's not that user friendly."

You must give whatever it is that you

want. If you want love you must give love, if you want trust you must trust someone. If you are down, cheer up someone else. This is how life works and there are no shortcuts, tips or tricks. The tip is to get to work on you. If you are overweight, eat less, move more. If you are shy, start watching funny movies and study the outgoing, funny guy, practice being like him or her a little each day and you can change your whole life. I always thought I was cool and funny, but my friends didn't think so. I started watching lots of funny movies because I wanted to be the guy who was popular at the party. Sure enough, after watching enough funny movies and studying the main character I learned to have a quicker sense of humor. Then I became the funny, popular guy and that was cool for a while until I realized it was all about me. Now I tell jokes and I goof around only at certain times to liven up the party or to rescue someone from embarrassment. I use comedy to ease situations or cheer someone up.

I think what makes me the happiest now is getting people to laugh and inspiring people through my daily actions. I lead by example. I'm human and I make mistakes and my leaders know that. The most important thing is that you are honest with your leaders. Don't pretend to be anything you're not, they will know. Your team knows you better than you know you.

Have you ever gone to one of your company's conventions? All you have to do is look around; you don't even have to talk to anyone to read their energy. You can just see that some people are leaders. They walk and stand with confidence.

Others you can see have a fake confidence. Some people walk around looking lost and confused, others have anxiety. Without even talking to you, people judge you. Although that will never change, it's not what you say it's who you *are* because you can't hide your body language. If I talk to you and you tell me how excited you are about your business, but your eyes keep dropping and your voice shakes even once, I can see, as anyone can, that you are lacking belief. You do not have the blue energy we were just talking about earlier. How long will it take to get this energy you ask? Not long, I say, but not overnight either.

I'm sure you have heard this, "You can't change your destination overnight but you can change your direction." My friend Matt Morrow says it often. He is one of the most brilliant people I know. He has mastered the basics.

Pay Attention

I was just listening to Tony Robbins talk about Coach John Wooden. My brother and I had the good fortune of meeting Coach John Wooden.

He invited us to his house and he spent 2 hours with us, talking about life and the fundamentals. How did we get this invitation? We had never met Coach Wooden before. This is where being ready and fully present pays off.

My brother and I went to a seminar in Anaheim where several very famous athletes were speaking. One of Coach Wooden's players gave Coach Wooden's home phone number out on stage as a joke, he did it very fast thinking nobody could possibly get it. Well, that guy didn't plan on my brother and I being there with our journals open. I wrote down part of it, but I didn't get all of it. My brother wrote down part of it, but didn't get all of it, but wouldn't you know it, he got what I missed and I got what he missed and we called Coach John Wooden that day.

We told him we had been in the front row wearing suits and we wrote down his number and we wanted to hang out with him. He was impressed and said yes, I'd love to meet the two brothers that were sitting in the front row wearing suits, taking notes.

We got to spend 2 hours with Coach Wooden at his condo in Westwood. He has passed on now, but he is still "The Wizard of Westwood." He was famous for getting great players to be better. That's not easy to do. Tony Robbins in his *Personal Power Program* talks about how mastery of the basics is how you really advance.

A big trap we sometimes fall into is we want to learn new stuff. I'm telling you it's not a better script or a nicer car that you need, it's just that you need to work on yourself.

One final thought on energy is that we all absorb energy, so it's critical that you pay attention to who you are around. So many people live in negative households, they have a negative roommate or family member. Jim Rohn says you can't just X everyone out of your life, but you can limit the time you spend with certain people, as they will greatly affect your energy. Whenever I'm somewhere where I'm feeling negative energy I excuse myself. It's hard enough to change ourselves, it's 10 times harder trying to change other people, and pointless anyway. Psychology 101: you can't change anyone but yourself. Some people are so addicted to their negative thinking, not only can you not help them, but they will drain you.

Take a break, go for a walk, write, listen to something positive, go watch a movie. There was a period in my life where my brother and I, even though we had always been close, were not getting along. We had to learn to take time outs and separate for a while until we were both in a better place. I promise you building a big team will take all your energy and you can't afford to hang out in negative environments.

Some relationships are toxic and you need to break away from them completely, some people are OK to hang around once in a while, but you can't live with them and other people want the best for you and inspire you. Remember Jim Rohn's observation that influence is two things: it's subtle and it's powerful. We don't end up off track right away but it happens over time because negativity gets absorbed by us, as does positive energy. So really work on spending time with the positive people and excusing yourself from negative spaces.

It's amazing how fast people can read your energy and it's funny people think they can hide it. Everyone can tell if you're on track or not, so the sooner you start working on yourself the sooner your handshake will get better and your eye contact will be stronger leaving your impressions better.

We have talked about a lot in this book

but don't think because we scratched the surface in a few chapters that you are an expert on any of them as I am still learning more about them everyday. The very act of learning keeps you sharp. Once you ripen, you rot.

People say, "Oh, I have heard all this before." My response is, "Oh yeah? You have also showered before, have you not? Yet you continue to do that daily…we can only hope."

If you want to be a leader and if you want to do well you must stay in the zone. You do that by reading and listening to positive things at least every other day, but daily is best.

People ask me how I got rich. When I tell them I listened to Jim Rohn, they say, "That's it?" I say "Well, that's where I started." It all starts with 1 positive act moving forward in the right direction. Don't let all the things you can't do stop you from the things you can do. You have to do what you can with what you have right now or you will never make it.

The tools and resources you need never show up all at once. You have to work and move forward with faith and every few steps you take lead you to the next mission and more tools will fall into your hands.

You Can't Fly With Wet Wings

Stay emotionally tough. There is a book called "Think and Grow Rich" by Napolean Hill and he says the number 1 thing you need to get rich is harmony in human relationships. So don't fight with people. Make up with your enemies or move away from them. Building a business while arguing with your girlfriend, wife, brother or whoever will be like trying to fly with wet wings. It's IMPOSSIBLE. You need all your strength to help others with their problems, so you cannot be focused on your personal problems 24/7.

So many people took advantage of me, lied to me, failed me, tricked me and worse, but I always bounced back. The only person that can really hurt you is you. How you talk to yourself is the most important thing. How you process feedback and rejection is so critical to your success. When people say no to me I say that's OK. I don't think they are stupid, and I don't waste time trying to convince them. I move on because I can work faster with 2 that want to go, than 10 that I must drag. Keep your eyes focused at the top of the mountain and realize every challenge that God or the Universe throws at you is one you can overcome.

You can go through it, over it, under it, or around it...every time.

Chapter 8
From Zero to Hero… Again

The most common question I get today is not how did I get rich back in my early days, but how did I build a team in South Africa from scratch, not knowing a soul? Well the answer is simple: I had to.

My mother used to say the only thing constant is change. Accepting this gives you two of the most essential skills in life: resilience and resourcefulness.

By 2000, I was on top of the world. For 5 years, my brother and I had enjoyed working 17-hour days (it's not work when you enjoy what you do), building the business, traveling the world. I decided to take a break and in 2009, I moved to Taiwan and sold half of my business.

Getting Through the Tough Times
I met and fell in love with Rebecca, a gorgeous model in Taiwan, but from Los Angeles like me. We lived together for 2 years and were planning on getting married.

She was the person that got me to start this book. She was a doer, not a talker and she would hit me every time I would exaggerate or talk about my past success.

She would always say, "OK, that's great, but it's in the past, what's next?"

"What's next" was this book. I wanted to give more than a one-line answer to the people who came up to me and asked what to do to be successful in this business. I just never found the time to do it.

In 2011, Rebecca passed away suddenly and tragically. I held her hand as the paramedics came. I talked to her, as she lay on the ground with her eyes open, still breathing. I told her she would be OK. She died in the hospital 4 hours later. It was and still is by far the most painful experience of my life. She was the one girl I finally saw myself marrying. I hated God and the world and blamed myself. I had horrible panic attacks and anxiety, I couldn't eat nor sleep and I couldn't figure out why this had happened.

With her encouragement, I wrote most of this book while Rebecca was alive and then stopped writing after her death. It took several years, but I'm finally finishing this book.

Rebecca made me a better person. She was the purest, most amazing person I had ever met. Everything was black or white with her. Nothing was grey.

After losing Rebecca, I flew to East Africa to stay with Clay Jackson for 2 months. In Mombasa, Kenya, I cried and drank for 2 months straight. I had really a hard time breathing. I couldn't sleep or eat or have normal conversations with people. I was seriously broken.

Eventually I had had enough of drinking and crying and yelling at God. When Clay asked me if I wanted to be the Country Manager of South Africa, my first reaction was "No."

He said, "Look, just go check it out. "I did and I said, "Just send my stuff over; I'm not going back to Kenya."

I moved to South Africa not knowing a single person and having no car. I lived in a hotel that Clay had purchased for a year. In less than a year, I built a team to over 3,000 members and I still had my existing team back in the United States.

The only reason I am sharing such a personal story with you is to let you know we all have problems, but we must get through them. I put one foot in front of the other and no matter what you are dealing with, so can you.

I slowed down the drinking and started going to the gym twice a day. I prayed for an hour a day and listened to Tony Robbins for an hour a day. I knew Rebecca would want me to get back on the horse and stop feeling sorry for myself. So many times I was doing a meeting for someone or for a group of people and I would be having a horrible panic attack but I couldn't show it. I looked calm on the outside but I was freaking out on the inside. I miss Rebecca everyday and I think about her family everyday. I pray for her, I pray for them, and I pray for myself.

Every time I would have a bad panic attack or anxiety I would say in my head, "Dear Jesus, hold me, guide me, walk beside me."

Every time, I would feel better. I'm not an overly religious person and I don't often go to church, but I can tell you without a doubt I know there is an angel in heaven helping me and I know there is someone up there or out there looking out for you, too. We can overcome anything and we can do more than survive, we can thrive. We can be happy and we can inspire others to do the same.

I believe we are all here to learn to work together and help each other. I don't know what you are going through in your life right now but you can get through it and you can have it all. I love you, pray for you and I look forward to meeting you.

When I landed in South Africa, as I already shared with you, I had been traveling the world for several years and sold half my business, so I was basically back at Zero financially and in many ways. I was heartbroken and had severe anxiety attacks. I was living in a hotel and I had no car. I was living in a country where I didn't know a single person.

To add yet another twist in the story, I went skydiving to cheer myself up and broke my leg in half and my ankle in 3 places. I was in a public hospital in a foreign country for 1 month and had 3 surgeries. I was the only white person I saw in the hospital and the nurses seemed to hate me. There were nights they didn't give me my pain medicine and I would lie awake all night in pain. I had a lot of time to think in that hospital.

I thought about my life and all the wrong choices I had made. I thought about Rebecca a lot and how much I missed her. I thought about my brother and how I missed being partners with him and working together. I thought about how much I missed my family and friends back home. The one thing I learned in the hospital that month was that nobody was going to come and rescue me.

Every old cliché I ever heard came to me,

"If it is to be, it is up to me." Rich people that made it from the bottom to the top are tough because they had to be tough to get there.

I finally got out of the hospital and back to my hotel. My mom almost begged me to come home so she could take care of me. She'd made the same offer after Rebecca died. My dad had come out to visit and I talked with both of them on Skype. I knew I had family who were there for me, but I needed to do this alone.

The painkillers were like a gift from God, I was taking 2 or 3 times as much as I was allowed per day. It took the pain away from my leg and helped me not think so much. I ran out of pain pills very quickly and was back to the pharmacy. The first 2 times the pharmacist refilled my order with no problem. The 3rd time I saw him look at me with apprehension.

He eventually stopped filling my prescription and I went through the worst depression ever. I spent about a month in my hotel room watching TV, feeling sorry for myself. I toughed it out and got off the pills and hit the gym twice a day.

You know what's funny? It's so easy to have these moments where you say, "OK enough is enough I'm going to kick ass now!" I said that to myself so many times, but didn't do it. However, this time enough was really enough. I thought about my options in life, what would I do if I wasn't doing Social Marketing? I thought about how many people I taught the business to, who are now off making way more than me. It was pretty depressing. The worst thought for me though was by far the thought of going and getting a job. If I went home I knew that's what my mom would encourage me to do. I thought about going on an interview, I thought about having co-workers and being late one day then getting yelled at by a boss.

The thought of getting a job scared me into action. I had a conversation with myself that went something like this, "Clif, you have made millions, you know what to do, go do it." So I got out of my hotel room, I ate out for breakfast, lunch, and dinner and started meeting people. They would all ask me why I came to South Africa and the whole answer would be too sad, so I told them I just came to take a break, which was also true. A good friend of mine, David Neil, said something I will always remember, "We all have to learn to be economical with our explanations." People don't need to know everything right away. I think young people have a problem with this, they explain too much too fast. As we get older we learn to hold some things back.

The start of my new life, my new team and my amazing comeback story – (he said with a smile and a hint of sarcasm) started with a guy named Jodi Taylor. He was the hotel night manager and he offered to drive me around. The hotel was owned by Clay, the guy I previously mentioned in my upline whose idea it was for me to come stay there. Jodi was and is a super intelligent guy, maybe one of the sharpest guys I have ever met. Very deep and intuitive. He was a high-powered corporate guy who had a nervous break down, and now lives in the hotel and drives guests around for extra cash. The more I talked to him the more impressed with him I became. We had many deep conversations about life, the world and ourselves.

I think hanging out with Jodi really helped me a lot. He helped me rebuild my confidence. He kept telling me how smart I am and how I was destined for greatness. He explained to me that South Africa is the perfect place for me and my skill set because South Africa has so many people in it ready to do something, but nobody to lead them. There are many "Aha!" moments on the way to success, but this was a big one.

He drove me around and helped me meet people. The first person that joined my team was a guest from the hotel who I met that asked me about the product. I keep my answers short and smile a lot. I try to be a good listener and only answer the questions the other person is asking. I also try to guide them to ask the right questions. Long story short, she joined, then did nothing and quit. This kind of thing went on for a while. Clay gave me $50.00 to set up a booth at a nearby mall and he wanted me to work the booth, pour drinks for people and have them sample the product. I could sell it there or just get people's phone numbers and follow up with them.

I remember my ego popping up every few hours the first few days. My ego would say to me, "What the hell are you doing?" You have made millions and now, here you are working a booth." Then an image in my head popped up of an old friend of mine David Wagner. This guy was always smiling and having a good time. It's funny how you meet so many people in life and you have so many experiences with them, but then you end up really remembering them for one thing. The one thing I remember David Wagner from Newport Beach for was his big smile and positive attitude.

So I smiled and told jokes and worked the crap out of my $50.00 booth every weekend. I got one rep from all that hard work and that one rep never grew into anything. But it got me out and meeting people and learning how they think. Funny thing about building a business in another country is they all look up to the US a little, but they kind of don't like us at the same time. They often think we are arrogant and that we feel we are the best.

The truth is we all love our countries and we are really not that different. Once you get to know them and show them you are not arrogant then they end up being your best friends. I learned how to take jokes about America, but stick up for America if they went too far. Now this has nothing to do with America or South Africa, I'm just talking about general conversation. You have to learn how to be bold, but not cocky. You have to be strong, but not a jerk.

Nothing really ever came from me working the booth, but that's OK – when you have nothing to do and no warm market, then doing anything is good because it gets you out and about. The more you do, the better off you are. Sitting around thinking all day will kill you. One day after the market, Jodi offered to take me to a beautiful restaurant called Bloomendale. We drove to the top of a hill that was surrounded by vineyards.

We got a table outside and ordered a

bottle of wine. The funny thing was that because we both used to be highly successful, we carried ourselves well, and whoever met us just figured we were doing well! I never have a plan when I'm socially recruiting, I just go out and meet people and try to make friends without looking like that's what I'm trying to do. The waitress wasn't interested, but she introduced us to the manager who would later become my top producer. It was on our way out that we met her.

Stella has bright red hair and is full of energy, very busy and always doing something. The perfect person I thought to myself. It took me like 2 weeks of going back in and ordering food or wine to finally get her to sit with me for a few minutes. I was with Jodi of course and he asked her if she was having a Braai any time soon. I jumped in and said, "What's a Braai?" They explained that a Braai was like an American BBQ, but on an open wood fire with steaks and sausages and all kinds of meats. I think their exact words were, "It's like BBQ but a million times better."

I was nervous, I felt like a kid going to the first day of school. Jodi took me to the grocery store and helped me pick out some good meat and bread and the right bottle of wine to bring over. I told her not to go too expensive or too cheap. Too expensive and you look like a show off because they don't know you yet, and too cheap, well that never looks good because wine is very cheap in South Africa to begin with!

I remember Jodi dropping me off and leaving. I remember the door shutting and then it was just me and a bunch of strangers. I must say they made it easy on me, after a few glasses of wine we were best friends. Stella introduced me to her daughter and her friends and we talked about everything, but my business. I really made it a goal to not be "that guy". I never avoided talking about it, but I kept all my answers very short. I have spoken about this a few times now in this book because it's what I do and it works. If you give people short, confident answers and you move on in the conversation, the right people will come along. They always do. There is no technique that works every time on everyone. You have to talk to lots of people to find the right people so have fun while you're doing it.

I like people and I like wine, so most of my recruiting was done over wine or dinners with people. At one point in the evening Stella told me she would join and buy the product and that she knew lots of people. I remember how excited I was, but how I tried not to show it too much.

90% of recruiting is timing. Later that week Stella told me she had been the manager of Bloomendale and girlfriend to the owner for 10 years that they were breaking up and she wanted to do something else. She explained to me how so many network-marketing companies had done events at the restaurant but they never appealed to her. She said I just happened to bring it up to her at the right time and she was ready.

Stella and I worked together like magic. I told her all she had to do was introduce people to me, tell them I had built a business in America and was in South Africa visiting. When people introduce you, have them keep it short and truthful. People don't want or need to know your whole life history, just the Clif Notes.

Stella was really an answer to my prayers. Many nights I thought to myself that Rebecca led me to Stella through Jodi and through Clay who invited me to South Africa. It's really crazy how things come together in the most random ways that you would never see coming. If you keep trying, have faith, and then invest your feelings into your day long enough, something good will happen. I was lucky to meet Stella so early on. The first 60 days were very slow and Clay asked me what was going on. We had a few fights over my production or lack thereof, but then I met Stella and business really took off.

The way we built it up was simple. You bring people; I do the meeting. Some people joined on the spot and some joined the next day, but it seemed like everyone she was bringing to me was jumping on. Most of our meetings were over coffee or wine and never exceeded 30 minutes, however we may have hung out with them longer if it was in a social environment. Stella quickly started doing meetings on her own too. Once you get the right person who is motivated like Stella they just pick up and run with it. We also took lots of trips together and she showed me all over South Africa. It was really amazing timing, we both needed a friend and we both needed to make money fast.

I became really good friends with her ex-boyfriend, Freddy Turner, who was the owner of Bloomendale restaurant. We signed up lots of his friends, too. He and I became really good friends and hung out a lot. I'm really very lucky I met Stella and Freddy and I'm thankful for that every day.

As you know you can't sit on top of one team for too long. You have to lead by example, frontline recruit, and stay sharp. Don't fall into the famous management trap

Mark Yarnell talks about. I would say on average I pass out 5-10 cards a day. I'm blown away when I hang out with other people in Social Marketing that don't do that. I'm able to have such a chill attitude with people and not care if they call me back or not, because I pass out so many cards a day. Most people are scared to talk to people so they over talk the business to their poor victim...I mean prospect.

I'm like a duck, calm on the surface but peddling like crazy underwater. I have a very serious work ethic with a casual style on the surface. Matt Morrow is probably the best in the world at that. He's always having fun and looks relaxed, but he's always recruiting. Matt and I never look like we are recruiting but we are, I think that's our magic. Once people can see that you want them, they want you less. Human nature. It's an art really because you don't want to come across as arrogant either. I'm good at having fun and keeping one eye open for business 24/7.

My next big leader in South Africa came from another restaurant manager. By this point I had learned how to drive on the left side of the road and on the left side of the car, shifting was a trick, but I was doing meetings all over town and couldn't rely on Jodi for everything. In South Africa you can't buy alcohol on Sundays, but you can order it at a restaurant on Sundays.

My whole life was about to change again and I didn't know it. It was a Sunday afternoon and I was in my hotel room, which by the way was a decent room overlooking a golf course. Can't complain about that! There was nobody on the team that needed a training or a meeting done for them, so I decided to go to a nearby restaurant called Lemon Butter, a nice restaurant inside the shopping mall I was working the booth at before I got my team up and running.

I drove to Lemon Butter and ordered a glass of wine and some sushi. I was totally broke, but I'm single with no kids and no bills, so what the heck right? I wanted to look the part. I did a lot of meetings where I felt like I was selling a dream and living a nightmare. Plenty of trainings were done by me on an empty stomach.

I remember seeing a very cool, older guy there who I thought was the owner, I remember watching him greet all the customers and I was jealous. I thought he owned the place and his life was perfect. He finally came up to me and asked how I was and I told him I was great of course – I asked him if he owned the restaurant and he laughed and said, "I wish!"

He told me he was the manager and then he asked what I did. I like to switch up my recruiting style now and again so I said, "Well I'm in network marketing." The smile ran off his face and he said, "Oh that's a bunch of Kak." then he walked off. He came back a few minutes later and apologized. He said he had tried network marketing a few times but never had success with it. He asked me if I made good money doing it, I smiled and said, "Yes I have."

He asked about the product and I told him about it with short answers as always. He asked me to bring some samples by sometime. Take note - the whole time we were talking, I was scanning the room to make sure customers were not getting angry that he was spending too much time with me. I'm always aware of my surroundings, you don't want your prospect to get in trouble, and you don't want to be that zombie Social Marketing person who won't shut up. Try to be normal when you are recruiting! I know we are all weird at times, but when you are recruiting that's the time to be your best.

I came by 2 days later and dropped off some samples. He paid me no attention and I wrote him off in my mind. A few days later I was back there for sushi not even thinking about him and he came up to me and said his back pain was all but gone and he was feeling great. I was so excited but tried to stay calm. I smiled and said, "Yeah, man! It's good stuff, huh?" He asked how much it was and I told him. He signed up the next day. We became really good friends. Neil is just a very well-adjusted guy, socially. He doesn't try to look younger than he is, but he is very hip. He doesn't try to impress people, but he knows wine in and out. He's just a really good guy.

Remember way back, like 2 paragraphs ago when I said my life was about to change? Well, Neil never became one of my top guys, although we are still very good friends today. He actually ended up quitting and doing well in a different Social Marketing company, but not before he introduced me to his best friend, Alan Boswell.

Alan was not an easy sell. I get to his house and it's very nice, with a big pool and his girlfriend, Nicky was there with him. The big difference between people in LA and people in Cape Town, South Africa is that people in South Africa will call you out if something doesn't sound right. They are very tough people and not afraid of verbal confrontation. It took some getting used to. Once I understood that their questions were not attacks, just concerns, then I was all-good. Alan owned a cell phone company and was earning residual income already so he got the concept right away.

I explained to Alan and his girlfriend how I had made lots of money in the past, but I was no longer rich. I explained to them that I still had a residual check that paid all my bills and that I didn't need to work; but I never tried to pretend I was super rich now. Honesty is always the best policy. You can't build good personal or business human relationships without it.

Alan and Nicky joined, and they introduced me to the who's who of Cape Town, the major restaurant and bar owners, liquor distributers and gym owners. It was just like working with Stella, our sign-up ratio was so high. Now I had 2 teams rocking and rolling. My check was finally going up again and I was getting my mojo back.

The whole time I was working, meeting people and doing meetings I just said to myself, "Have faith this will all work out." I pictured the end result and I held it in my mind. People came and went. I never get attached to how I'm going to do something, I just get attached the end result of it happening. I built and lost a lot of business in America, I built a team that fell apart in Taiwan, and now there I was in South

Africa.

All I know is that if I try hard enough, long enough, and I stay open to coaching from people that I look up to, I will make it. I spent a lot of time with Alan and his friends, we signed up a lot of people and we had a lot of fun, but as Tom Alkazin always says, "It's not about getting them in, it's about getting them going."

The challenge I faced with these guys is that they were all fairly wealthy already and it was hard to get them to come to training, or even to set up a training session at their house.

So one day I was at Alan's house doing a meeting for some friends of his and his son walks in. His son, Graedon, is a DJ, a model, and a total hippie. I could never have predicted it, but Graedon ended up being my top producer and big team #3!

You can't get comfortable with 1 big team or 2; you need at least 3 if not 4 or 5. When we met, Graedon was too cool for school and not interested at all. He walked in the house said hi to his dad. We met briefly, then he was out the door.

Alan and I decided to go to his friend's nightclub, because he had just joined Vemma as well and we could chat for a bit. So we went and met up with James, the owner of 2 very popular clubs in Cape

Town. James is such a star, everyone loves him and he is the life of the party. I thought to myself…the next Stella! Never happened. James joined and liked the product, but was busy focused on opening his 3rd bar. 90% of recruiting is timing, remember? We all walked up to the bar and Alan's son, Graedon was bartending. Again, nothing happened. Graedon showed no interest.

Eventually, Graedon sat in a meeting and decided to join, then he did nothing for 2 months. Slowly, he started getting more involved, showing up more often and asking questions. He said he was getting tired of working late nights as a DJ and bartender. I remember being in the car with Clay, who is usually in East Africa and he said to me, "I think there is something about Graedon, you should really take him under your wing." I agreed and that was the beginning of my massive Young People Revolution (YPR) team.

We have enrolled over 4,000 kids in South Africa and we enroll something like 50 college students a day there. Our meetings are 100-300 people, about 5 nights a week. The meetings feel like parties, the energy is high and people are excited to come.

So, how did this happen? Well, there are 3 stages to building a team.

CREATE MOMENTUM – Enthusiasm

SUSTAIN MOMENTUM – Organized System

ADVANCE MOMENTUM – Training and Duplication

CREATE

In the beginning you have to take every meeting and every call. You agree to everything. Just ordered pizza and took the first bite? When the phone rings, put the pizza down. People call you when they are ready to talk. You finish your pizza, call them back and now they may be at their house eating pizza and they don't answer the call. Someone calls and asks you to do a meeting across town in 10 minutes, no problem. I drove 2 hours to meet with one girl. She joined, then enrolled her parents and friends and built a nice sized team. Had I said no, it's too far, or maybe next week I would have lost her.

SUSTAIN

You can't keep up this kind of schedule forever, or you will red line it. You have to switch gears and make people start coming to you, but not until the rpm's are high enough. If you switch gears too soon the car will slow down or worse yet, die.

Momentum is everything. Once you can't possibly keep up the pace, you switch gears and create a schedule. I made my meetings every Tuesday and Thursday for this young team, but we couldn't get the energy level up so we cancelled Thursdays and just did Tuesdays. Once we got Tuesdays packed, then we re-opened Thursdays. The real key to success with this team was training. The great thing about college kids is they are used to taking notes and I am very comfortable in front of a room.

ADVANCE

You advance momentum through training and duplication. When you recruit and train someone it's like you performed a magic trick on them, they don't know how you did it, but they liked it. You have to tell them to watch you perform the magic on someone else now, so they can really pay attention and watch what you do from another angle. You have to teach to teach to teach.

I treat my first 100 reps like I personally enrolled them, but I don't do meetings for my leaders. I make them watch me do it. You have heard the old saying, "Give a man a fish and you feed him for a day, teach a

man to fish and you have feed him for life."
Same deal. You gotta push your little birds
out of the nest at some point. I usually tell
my new people they have 6 weeks under my
wing.

For weeks I will do all the meetings and
trainings for them if they are with me to
watch and take notes. So they must pay
attention because by week 7, I expect them
to be able to do their own meetings. Have I
ever broken this rule? Yes all the time, but
it's a good basic rule to have that I mostly
follow. If some guy just isn't getting it but
he keeps bringing me A+ people I will keep
working with him until I get one of those A+
people to run with me. Rules are made to
broken, I break them all the time, but I never
did that until I was making $100K a month.

We did meetings every Tuesday and
Thursday with trainings every Saturday.
They started small and awkward with lots of
skeptical people. But once we got a few
people on board, they came to training and
their belief was strengthened. Then we had a
few cheerleaders in the room. I trained
everyone to pay attention and lean forward. I
said, "Look, I have made a sh#t load of
money and I'm here to help you guys. Do
you want your friends to join or be bored,
then go home?" They said, "Join of course"
and I said, "Good, so lean forward and smile

and laugh at all my stupid jokes, help me help you." They agreed and our meetings took off. Graedon was a sponge calling me 10 times a day. He's texting me now while I write this.

Why did Graedon decide to follow me? Why did Stella decide and why did Alan decide along with Neil and many others? Why? Because they can see I'm not full of BS. When you are new, people might not follow you so you must get good at using company tools, like a video and 3-way call. You may not live near the meetings or home office but if you get good prospects interested someone in your upline will talk to them.

My pitch now to people is "Hey, come follow me! I'm on fire!" Before that it was, "Hey, let's work together", and before that it was "Hey come meet my friend who has made lots of money." You have to know your cards and play them well.

Today people follow me. My check is growing, my team is rank advancing. I'm the guy that put South Africa on the map for Social Marketing, so people listen to me. There isn't any other Social Marketing company in the whole country doing meetings like me, with as many people, 5 nights a week. My point is until you're the man, don't try to be. In the beginning you have to follow a leader.

Follow the Leader

Find someone who is where you want to be and work hard to earn their attention. Don't complain. If your team does crappy conference calls, then plug into another teams' calls. If your team has crappy meetings, then plug into someone else's. If you can't find any good meetings or training to plug into, then you might have to start doing your own, but just don't act like you are a big shot, that's the wrong hand to play for now. I have been rich and lost it a few times and the cool thing about losing it all is that you fall down and learn to relate with people again. When you have a Lamborghini and 4 other cars, all new top models, then it's easy to recruit. When you live in the Hollywood Hills and you sell out trainings of 3K, 5K and 10K people, you are on fire and it takes very little effort to recruit.

When you are at the bottom you have to use your heart. My pitch was, "Dude, I'm doing this because I'm sick and tired of being sick and tired. I don't want my mom to have to work. I hate going to the restaurant, looking at the menu, wanting steak and ordering fries."

If you lead with your heart, people will

follow. You just have to know where you are and play the cards you have. If you act like a big shot when you are not, nobody will follow you. You will get weird, have no friends and die alone. OK, I went too far on that one, but you get it.

You can't learn everything all at once. There is so much I want to share with you, but one step at a time. Going back to the original question of how I built a team from scratch in South Africa is simple: I had to.

"Rock bottom became the solid foundation on which I re-built my life."

I truly believe we can do the impossible, because I have been through what to me was the unimaginable, losing my fiancée.

Within the same few years of losing Rebecca, I lost my best friend and business partner, my house, my cars, my reputation, and almost lost my leg. I had nowhere else to go but up.

Do you have to lose it all like I did? No.

Would it get you going? Hopefully.

Diamonds are created by extreme heat and pressure. Anthony Robbins says pressure makes you or breaks you. He says people change because they get inspired or desperate. Don't wait to hit the bottom. Let my story and the stories of others inspire you. The magic you think you need is already inside of you.

There is nothing you need except to change the story in your head about how hard things are for you and find a way to win. Read the books, listen to the tapes, find a coach, work hard to deserve his or her attention, be coachable, then put what you learn into action.

You are the magic.

Special Thanks to: Dave Braun, Matt & K.C. Morrow, Clay Jackson, BK, Nathan Curran, Robert Roa, my Parents, Genie Gastelum, Piper and Ina All my new friends in South Africa, my Taiwan friends and everyone I have ever worked with. Special thanks to Enrique & Nicole for believing in me.

About the Author

Clif Braun is widely recognized as one of the most inspirational, entertaining, and authentic leaders in the world of Social Marketing. He has been full time in the home-based business field since he was 19 years old. Clif is committed to helping people achieve their full potential and travels the world pursuing his passion for speaking on stage and working closely with his teams on the ground.

Currently, Clif spends half his time in his new favorite city of Capetown in South Africa, and the other half in the USA. If you would like to follow Clif, you may do so at any of the following:

@clifbraun = twitter
@clifbraun = Instagram
Facebook.com/clifbraun
YouTube.com/mrclifbraun

Made in the USA
San Bernardino, CA
29 April 2016